Beyond Prayer and Praise

A Spiritual Memoir

MANGAL BIHARI

BEYOND PRAYER AND PRAISE
ISBN - 978-1-4477-2605-0

Press
1/10 Malviya Nagar, Jaipur 302017, India
www.mangalbihari.com
Cover design: Kalyanii Bihari

For bulk order prices or any other inquiries, please contact
contact@mangalbihari.com

For my most beloved Baba

Foreword

A Spiritual Journey for All

I read this book on my i-phone. With ease, I carried Mangal Bihari's spiritual memoirs wherever I went. Whenever I have had some free time, I eagerly returned to his life story. For many days, this book became a dear friend. But the impressions Bihari's memoirs have left with me will last many many years.

Reading them, I feel waves of peace come over me. But this is not a tale of endless yogic miracles, rather a story of staying in bliss even while the world around us changes. And the world has changed. Writes Bihari in the first chapter: 'My primary education was in government managed rural schools of the erstwhile western Indian states of Jhalawar and Kota. Every day we had to blacken with coal dust our wooden slates and dry them in the sun and wind in order to write upon them in white with a wooden pen. Almost half the school time was used in this operation'. Contrast this with 2011 and i-books.

However, Bihari's book is not just about social and technological change, but about that part of us that does not change. Even as a baby he knew that he was never alone, that the 'Great' was with him. Says Bihari: 'The first vivid memory of my infancy is that I am lying face up in the soft sands of a small river. There are pools of water, light green, on either side of me. The water is not frightening, but pleasantly cool and my mother is bathing in one such pool with some other ladies. I cannot see them, but I feel their reassuring presence. This was perhaps my first awareness of consciousness in this life'.

It is in 1958, while reading the Gita, he came to the following lines: 'Know that I am the one and only knower in all fields'. Bihari reveals: 'As I read these lines, the knower within me became 'me' in a mysterious manner, and instead of being the reader, I became the knower. I was lost in a higher state of consciousness. My 'me' became Krishna, the all-knowing entity. I cannot describe that experience in words. It was the first time in my life that I had a glimpse of my innermost self'.

The book thus has two strands. One is an intimate account of his life story — when he married, his illustrious career in the Indian Administrative Service, the professional challenges he faced in a changing world — and the second are his spiritual experiences, the timeless part of his life. These are encounters with his deepest inner most self, whom he would later ascribe to his 'Baba' — his spiritual teacher, Shrii Shrii Anandamurti.

Both aspects of this book are central to the overall story. From his family and career life, we see a man who while working, while being a good husband, father, and grandfather, did his duty. He lived the ethical and purposeful life. From his narrations of meeting with Anandamurti, we learn of devotion, of love, of meetings with a remarkable man, who remained always in presence, always in Bliss.

He describes one scene when he meets a Mr Prasad, a senior officer in Indian customs. Writes Bihari: 'I asked him why he was weeping when he saw Baba. "Don't bother", he replied, "you will also weep one day"'. And Baba's bliss does touch him and his wife. Bihari adds: 'We stayed on in the blistering heat of Jamalpur to witness the wonderful spiritual phenomenon that was my guru. We became attached to the small room where Baba used to meet his disciples morning and evening, to the field and the tiger's grave and to the hills, dales and lakes of Jamalpur and above all to the whole atmosphere of that place, where every day we received new experiences, more spiritual knowledge, more divine love and more and more of that subtle sweetness, which used to permeate our whole being there'.

Anandamurti provided a model to Bihari as to how to live the ideal life. Live in both worlds at the same time. Even when there is some discomfort, some physical or mental challenge, keep one eye on the spiritual even as one does one's work. We learn that the spiritual and family-career journey are not two different paths, two different narratives, but they are the same story.

Bihari has lived the integrated life. He has loved his family, loved his guru, and loved humanity. We are fortunate to have him as our guide, the light that inspires us to as well live an integrated balanced life — a life of prama, of Ananda. Read this book and let it become your friend, for now, and for life.

— Sohail Inayatullah, February 2011

Foreword

A Beautiful Storyteller

Although I knew Mangal Bihari somewhat during my early days as a whole-time worker of Ananda Marga, I really came to know him well during my posting in the US. I think he might have come to the US in the month of March in 1971 on some work as an Indian civil servant. He attended my meeting with graduate students at Harvard University and stayed with me for a day. During his visit to the US I invited him to give some talks on Ananda Marga philosophy at a couple of different venues. We had a number of wonderful conversations about our guru and his spiritual ideology.

Since then we have become good friends. I have felt his deep devotion for Baba and regard him as one of Baba's great devotees. He has a very helping nature and has always gone the extra distance to shoulder responsibilities for the Ananda Marga organization and the welfare of its workers.

I received initiation into Ananda Marga spiritual practice in 1965 and had my first personal contact with Baba shortly thereafter. I was immediately drawn to his magnetic personality and after the intensely blissful meditation experience I had in his presence, I was convinced that he is a supremely powerful spiritual force. As I cried full of devotion for him during that first meeting, he asked me to help the suffering humanity without fail and I responded positively.

I know that it is very difficult to put into words the intuitional experiences of a traveller on the spiritual path. Only through stories of able practitioners can we get glimpses of the nature of treasures that lie in wait along the journey. This book provides such a collection of stories and Mangal Bihari is a beautiful storyteller.

I sincerely wish that he stays with us many more years and guides spiritual aspirants who wish to know more about Baba. His stories about Baba will surely inspire anyone who yearns for spiritual direction in life.

— Dada Yatiishvarananda, March 2011

All quotes before chapters are from
Prabhat Ranjan Sarkar

That which makes the mind soft and strong and strenuous, so it may keep itself in a balanced state even in the condition of pain — that which perpetually creates a pleasant feeling within, is called love. Devotion is identical with love. The moment devotion is aroused, the love of God comes.

14 October 1966, Mumbai

Introduction

As I look back on my life at eighty years and more, I am thrilled to remember and describe the many elements of drama that filled those years.

On a midnight of *shravan*, when it was raining cats and dogs, I was born in a thatched hut of a hamlet of not more than sixty mud huts in the backward district of Jhalawar in western India. I came without the aid of a midwife. The midwife had to be brought on foot from a town about two to three kilometres away. By the time my maternal uncle returned with her, it was too late. A tribal messenger was sent to inform my father who was a village primary school teacher some ten miles away. It took the man two days to return home, as he had to swim at least three swollen rivers. During the rains the rivers used to acquire almost jet speed in their currents, with the result that the best of swimmers could only reach the other bank after being carried by the current some five or six kilometres downstream.

My primary education was in government managed rural schools of the erstwhile western Indian states of Jhalawar and Kota. Every day we had to blacken with coal dust our wooden slates and dry them in the sun and wind in order to write upon them in white with a wooden pen. Almost half the school time was used in this operation. The rest of the time, we were to cram tables and fables and poems. I wonder at the bulky school bags of modern day kids. Up until the fourth class I hardly had but a pencil and a small notebook. All our faces were generally blackened from preparing our small blackboards, almost as if it were our uniform. Having finished our writing and cramming, we were free to play in the school or outside without any restriction. Our games were the traditional *kabbaddi*, *khoh* and *gilli-danda*. The teacher would ring the bell at about the end of the day, as there were no watches or wall-clocks, not only in the school but perhaps in the whole town.

For my middle school, I had to live in a hostel, which consisted of the school's vacant rooms after the teaching day was over. We used to cook *dal* and *roti* for ourselves — the *dal* mostly watery and the *rotis* half-baked or burnt — but it did not harm our health. We loved our food, as the hunger was sharp. There was no ghee, butter, or cooking oil. Some of us did drink milk in the evening in a nearby sweet shop. Sweets prepared from milk were about sixteen kilos for a rupee, but where was the one *anna* to eat even one fourth of a kilo any day?

The middle exam, equivalent to eighth grade, was the end of education in those days in our part of India, enough to make one a teacher, or a local government official. Middle pass was a good passport for any decent job. Society respected people with middle pass and the government employed them. No one with a higher education was seen for hundreds of miles around.

Having completed my education thus, I was betrothed within the same caste to a girl of a comparatively richer family. Marriage in those days was overdue for a boy of fifteen or sixteen. My would-be in-laws suggested my being sent for matriculation to Baran, the nearest big town, and they agreed to subsidize the expenses to some extent. So I was admitted into Baran High School for a composite course in English and Matriculation. Unfortunately, my father expired the very next year, leaving my mother, three brothers, three sisters and a small debt. The elder brother of my father, who was a *Patwari* (land records officer) and was without children, took the orphaned family with him to our native village, Pachpahar — a lovely village-cum-town on the banks of a very small but perennial rivulet, surrounded by green hillocks.

I had the option either to become a village schoolteacher like my father or to continue further studies at my own cost and risk. On returning to the hostel in Baran, sympathetic teachers and the Principal arranged a tuition for me to continue studies. In fact, tuitions were my constant companions and financiers throughout my student career, culminating with a Master of Arts degree in English Literature. During every summer vacation I took up some job or appointment to supplement my resources for further studies. Thus, I was a Rationing Inspector in Kota (1942), a private tutor of the children of the Prime Minister of Cooch Behar (1946) and a private tutor of a big landlord of Kota (1942-44) and held many other part-time jobs in the intervals to earn as much as possible for the rest of the year.

On completing my Master's degree from St. John's College, Agra, and winning the Sheshadri Gold Medal for standing first in the then Agra University, I was offered no less than seventeen jobs of Lecturer in English without a single application from me. After brief trials in a few colleges, I preferred to settle down as a Lecturer in English in my home town of Kota. I dreamt of a flourishing academic career full of writings and research, honours and quick promotions. However, in the first instance of applying for promotion, I was ignored and a well-connected candidate of dubious academic merit was preferred. I was deeply hurt and took the next opportunity to get out of the academic field.

I was selected as an Income Tax Officer in the national civil service. A prolonged training before joining my post gave me a good peep into the world of business, accounting, audit and finance. I had hardly started in my new job when a special recruitment drive gave me another opportunity to change track in my career by joining the very prestigious Indian Administrative Services (IAS) with retrospective seniority.

In IAS, I held several coveted postings at the state level, for instance, as Head of Rajasthan State Electricity Board, Head of Rajasthan State Roads and Transport Corporation, and Rajasthan Finance Commissioner, among others. Later, I also served at the Government of India level as Deputy Director General Food and as Chief Director Sugar. My last posting at the national level was as Additional Secretary Defence, where unfortunately, two of my bosses, i.e. the Defence Secretaries, died in office. Therefore, for a long period I had to supervise the whole of India's Defence Department as its administrative head.

There was a historical fracture in my service during the Emergency (1975-77), when due to wilfully defying the orders and wishes of the then Prime Minister of India, Indira Gandhi, I had to remain away from service for nearly eighteen months, sans postings, sans pay and sans even an order whether I was on leave, suspension or dismissal. The government's infringement on civil rights and liberties of many people during this period has been well documented since.

After the Emergency period was over and Indira Gandhi was ousted from power, the Shah Commission was instituted to investigate the excesses committed by Gandhi's government. Perhaps, I was the only officer from the IAS to approach the Commission for suffering duress during the emergency under that regime; and the Commission devoted a chapter to me in their report, approving my stand and condemning the government of Indira Gandhi for what it had done to me.

My exit from the service was quite unceremonious, to say the least. The elected Rajasthan government wanted my services back in the state as Chairman of Rajasthan Public Services Commission after Indira Gandhi returned as Prime Minister. But I was not relieved from my position then and only thrown back to Jaipur when the state was under President's rule. My last posting as Commissioner Rehabilitation was a demotion and I was asked to vacate the official residence in less than a month of my retirement, even though I had no house of my own in Jaipur.

Nevertheless, there is a dramatic difference between the morning and evening of my life. I came from a nondescript small village, and from being an unknown entity in my formative years, I was widely known by the end of my fruitful career. After my retirement from government service, I continued an active public life, primarily as an op-ed columnist in Rajasthan Patrika, the Hindi newspaper with the widest circulation in Rajasthan at that time. My journalistic writings also appeared in various other newspapers. On occasions, I was appointed by respective state governments to chair commissions on policy-making as well as audit enquiries.

I have recollected my time in administrative service in my earlier book, 'Prashasanik Chintan', published by Rawat Publications, Jaipur.

In this book, however, my focus is not on my academic and professional career, but on a journey that has had a deeper meaning and salience in my life. Here I recall episodes and incidents that relate to the journey of my inner 'self', my spiritual journey. This journey owes everything to my guru, Shri Shri Anandamurtiji, the founder of the Ananda Marga mission. We disciples lovingly call him Baba, the most beloved one.

There is no such thing as 'supernatural' in this world. All sorts of powers lie dormant in human beings. Sometimes we get glimpses of these latent powers.

July 1960, Muzaffarpur

The Supernatural

Baba was constantly there. Even before he came into my life physically as my guru, he was knocking through the surface of my existence as a subterranean spring. On some occasions he would briefly stop the mad traffic of the external flow of my consciousness and let me peep at the totality of life. Many such moments and their joys have now been submerged in the pool of distant memories, but it is still possible to recall and reconstruct some of them.

Once, Baba hinted at some of my early spiritual experiences, reminding me that he was with me all along, right from my infancy. He has appeared in me as a vivid awareness of awareness, as one who led me on unmapped routes to undeserving success, to relief and to glimpses of bliss. These experiences were the milestones of my spiritual journey. Their significance lies in a gradually developing belief that I am never alone, that the Great is with me, whether or not I am always aware of him.

The first vivid memory of my infancy is that I am lying face up in the soft sands of a small river. There are pools of water, light green, on either side of me. The water is not frightening, but pleasantly cool and my mother is bathing in one such pool with some other ladies. I cannot see them, but I feel their reassuring presence. This was perhaps my first awareness of consciousness in this life. According to my mother, when I questioned her about it many years later, I must have been about eight or nine months old at that time.

Right from a tender age of seven or eight, I was doing some kind of worship and recitation of holy books. It was a habit imitated by me without any guidance. At the age of about twelve, a Brahmachariji (celibate monk) taught me to recite the mantra '*Tattvamasi*' (That thou art). I also learnt a bit from him about other yoga practices. As a boy from the *brahmin* caste, I was given a *yagyopavit* to wear. The priest who headed the ceremony, at which I received the sacred thread, was considered quite scholarly and religious in my native village of Pachpahar. During the ceremony he whispered in my ear the *Gayatri* mantra. This mantra is a prayer to the effulgent supreme power that pervades this universe to guide one's intellect on the righteous path. The priest wanted me to memorise this and recite it after bath every morning. I did this religiously throughout my early youth and adolescence. When I was married at the raw age of eighteen, I also taught this mantra to my wife, who was only sixteen at that time, but was eager to follow me on the spiritual path.

A mystical experience that belongs to my student days can possibly be called my first direct contact with the supernatural.

I had gone to Birla College, Pilani for my graduation in Arts. I was a hosteller. In the second year of my stay there, I contested the election for the post of College Union President and won it easily. In the very first month of my assuming charge, I decided to oppose, what I considered, was economic exploitation of the students by the college administration. One instance was the compulsory college uniform, white shirt and white trousers, which one had to buy only from the college canteen. I prepared a list of such other unreasonable restrictions and compulsions and served a notice to the college management to remove them. On refusal of our demands by the management, the whole college went on strike. I rushed from one hostel to another to enforce the strike and to interfere in cases of rough behaviour — whether by students or by the management.

In response to the strike, the Principal closed the college and rusticated me along with two or three other student leaders.

I returned home to Kota in a completely shattered mental condition. We hoped that by Diwali all punitive orders would be withdrawn and things would return to normal. But October came, and though classes resumed and other students were pardoned, I remained expelled.

So it looked to be the end of my studies and career. My finances were pitiable. The whole family depended on the income I received from scholarships and tuitions. My father had expired years ago and the family had no property or other income. It looked like my world had collapsed completely.

I was desolate and desperate and fell seriously ill with typhoid. The fever continued for over a month. My mother, my wife and my younger brothers and sisters all helplessly waited on the brink of catastrophe. There was no one to help, although many came to show their sympathies. There was neither money for treatment nor for the maintenance of the family.

As I was considered a brilliant student in that small town of Kota, the message of my plight and sickness reached the Chief Medical Officer of the State and he started visiting me free of cost. But in spite of the medicines and expert medical care, my condition continued to deteriorate. And then one sad evening Dr Saxena came to see me and declared that I was in a very critical condition and would most likely not survive the night.

It was the dark fortnight of the month and in my house, where there was no electric connection, the night became darker and darker. Children slept here and there without food. No meals were cooked that evening after the doctor's dismal statement and my mother and wife began to keep vigil at my bed in turns.

My mother had a rosary in her hands which was constantly on the move. She was exhausted and sat stooping and half wakeful on the verandah.

My wife was swooning in a corner of my bedroom. The tears from her eyes had dried up. Widowhood at less than twenty was a horrible prospect for a Hindu woman — enough to break her down completely.

It was nearly three or four in the morning. I was in a kind of deep stupor, only vaguely conscious of my surroundings and the impending catastrophe. Then I heard a soft voice asking me to get up. The words were repeated and became louder and more audible.

I was too weak to move, and yet I was being asked to sit up and stand. I mechanically obeyed this unknown voice and sat up in my bed. But the voice wanted me to stand up. I obeyed again. And surprisingly no special effort was needed in standing up, although I had been bed ridden and without solid food for more than twenty days. It appeared as though the voice that ordered also gave me the strength to obey.

I was then asked to walk along the bed and go to the earthen lamp that was throwing dim light into the room. I took some oil from the lamp and applied it to my dishevelled hair, combing through it. Then I picked up a knife and trimmed my nails, which had grown quite long. After doing all this, I came back to my bed and lay down again. I felt as though the whole room was filled with a cool blue light and it had a soothing effect on all my limbs and organs.

Then the thoughts of my financial state and my career returned and filled me with sadness. But in a divine way I was assured that I would never be deprived of the means to live. Whenever I would be in need, the means to fulfil that need would arise. And my career would also be on track again soon. These assurances gave me such a sweet tranquil feeling that I fell into a deep and peaceful slumber.

The next morning, my mother was the first to wake up and rushed to my bed. She was almost horrified to see me in such deep sleep. She gently awakened me. I told her that some divine force had relieved me of my sickness. As proof, I showed her my combed hair, my trimmed nails and my capacity to sit up, stand and walk. My wife soon joined us and everyone rejoiced without understanding what had actually happened. In about a week, I regained my hunger and strength.

In mid January news came that some of my colleagues had undertaken a hunger strike unto death for my sake in the temple at Vidyavihar, Pilani. Seth Jugal Kishore Birla, a great philanthropist, was in Pilani in those days and heard of this hunger strike undertaken by college boys. He was compassionate enough to call Pandeyji, our Principal, and ask him to revoke all punishment against me. Pandeyji readily agreed to call me back to the college.

The result was that I was back in Pilani by the 26th of January 1946 and began to prepare for the final B.A. exam. I studied very hard and passed the exam with flying colours winning the Mahadevi Bhai Gold Medal for standing first in the college.

This was my first encounter with death and danger and I got not only providential succour, but also an abiding faith in my destiny. I began to see life as a gift of the unknown power that had visited me that night to restore my physical and mental health and set me back on the rising road of my career. My optimism became robust and I felt that some superior power was guiding and protecting me.

With my friends in Kota where I took up my first job as a Lecturer in English Literature at Herbert College after finishing my postgraduate studies at St. John's College in Agra. I am first from the right.

From left: my brother Satya Bihari with my son Mukt, and my wife Sarla with my youngest son Gagan.

From left (middle row): Sarla, I, my mother, my eldest son Anand, and his wife Gita

He is the one who is the knower even of your sense of ego. Try to know Him.

1955, Jamalpur

The Knower

Before being initiated into Ananda Marga meditation, my *puja* was haphazard and desultory. It was a self-manufactured mixture of my family's traditional worship and my friend's sporadic advices, along with readings from some holy books. My father used to observe *Navratra*, nine days of special worship, twice in the year — once at the junction of the rainy and winter season, and then again during the transition from winter to summer. These nine days were considered especially propitious for meditation, worship and ritualistic pleasing of the gods and goddesses.

Traditionally we were worshippers of *Shakti*, the supreme energy. In fact, as the story goes, about one hundred years ago one of our ancestors was without children. So every day he used to walk some five to six miles to worship Durga, the goddess of supreme energy. He would walk to the temple without shoes, and there recite the whole *Durga Saptashati*, the seven hundred verses in honour of the Goddess. Only in the afternoon, on returning from the temple, would he take his sole meal of the day. It is believed that this penance finally resulted in a dream in which he was instructed to bring one of the idols from that temple to our village, install it in a beautiful place amidst groves of tall trees on the banks of the river and worship it there. He obeyed the dream and had children thereafter, who expanded into our big family of *Pandyas* (a clan within the *Brahmin* caste).

Since then all the members of the family used to worship Goddess Durga, daily or on special occasions at home and in the temples. I also picked up this practice. It was a worship to placate the Goddess to bestow material prosperity and respect in society on oneself.

In the beginning it used to take me more than two hours to recite all the seven hundred aphorisms of the *Saptashati*. But with practice, the time was reduced to about an hour. To start with, my mind would visualise the bloody wars the Goddess fought in her numerous incarnations with demons of various descriptions and powers. Over time however, the sanguine details became boring and I would recite them without imagining and in rapid routine. Sometimes a vague but beautiful sense would emerge from the mythical details. But I could not sustain it long. I used to think that these were only useful to the warriors of yore who fought with swords and spears. However, I did like the chapters that praised the divine qualities of *Shakti* and instructed on the prayers to be offered with surrender and devotion.

This one hour or so was supplemented, prefixed or suffixed, with recitations of other mantras such as the *Gayatri* mantra, the reading of at least two chapters of the Gita (the teachings of Lord Krishna) so that the whole book could be finished in nine days, and one out of nine chapters from Ram Charit Manas (the story of Lord Ram). This took another two to three hours.

I would repeat the *Gayatri* mantra at least one hundred and eight times. Here I found some sense as it was a prayer for the light of pure intellect and wisdom. Sometimes I would read *Gopal Sahastranam*, a thousand names of Lord Krishna. I wondered, though, how epithets such as deceitful, crooked and *rannchhor* (one who retreats from the battlefield) advanced the Lord's list of qualifications and qualities. On the other hand I felt that Krishna's personality was really charming and all-embracing.

The Gita always fascinated me. And as I had some smattering knowledge of Sanskrit, my readings from the Gita were always serious and thoughtful. New meanings and interpretations of verses would sometimes emerge and gladden my heart.

Readings from the Ram Charit Manas were a joy of another kind. It was like flowing through a rich river of emotion. From a literary point of view it was a pure delight. I could hardly hold my tears at critical junctions in the epic, although I had crossed these fields umpteen times. It was a real catharsis. My feeling of respect and admiration for Lord Ram was overwhelming at times. He was so strong, so virtuous, so handsome, so correct and so kind in his behaviour and attitude towards all.

In between these readings and recitations, I also paused for *dhyan*, a meditation in which I would visualise my favourite picture of Krishna. As a result of various suggestions from people, I would sometimes locate him in my heart region, sometimes on my forehead and at other times on the top of my head.

Before beginning my worship I would install pictures of Durga, Krishna, Shiva and Ram on a slightly raised platform, duly decorated with red silk. Flowers and incense played an important part in the practice and so did sandal paste, which I would apply to the pictures and idols in front of me as well as to my own forehead. I would normally sit wearing only a small loincloth and a scarf placed loosely over my shoulders. It was in a remote and lonely corner of the house that I sat like this for five to six hours every day.

I also used to do a *havan*, an offering in prayer through the use of fire and *ghee*, at the beginning of every worship. The ritual always ended with an *arti*, a prayer song, in which other members of the family would join me and offer food to the Gods. After *arti*, the food became *prasad*, imbued with holy vibrations. All present would take small pieces for their purification. Of course, the main lamp, made of cotton wicks in *ghee*, would remain burning uninterrupted for all the nine days and nights. The supplies of *ghee* were carefully supplemented by my wife. If the lamp were to be extinguished it would be treated as a bad omen. So all care was taken to save the flame from wind.

In the evening again I would sit for an hour or two and recite the *Gayatri* and other mantras, finishing off with *arti*. I had also become fond of *Ravankrit Shiva Stuti*, which is a poem in praise of Lord Shiva, and would loudly recite it towards the end of the evening worship. A picture of Lord Shiva sitting in snowy mountains adorned by waterfalls was one of my favourites.

Thus my practice of worship was like a sumptuous dinner with umpteen plates of different hues and tastes in an environment beautifully decorated with fragrant flowers and filled with the sweet smell of incense. The outcome was judged not only by spreading pleasantness in the mind and temper, but also by a subsequent rise in career and wealth, as well as an improvement of relations in the family and society. I wanted to believe that I was being more and more liked by the gods and goddesses. Like the emperors of yore, perhaps these gods and goddesses enjoyed the service mentally rendered to them, and the humility and flattery displayed during prayers.

But all this left me dissatisfied deep within. Questions arose in my mind about the existence and the 'divine' nature of the deities I was worshipping so devotedly. Moreover, this give and take with divinity was somewhat repugnant to my inner nature. What about those who did not pray? Were they entirely left to their dismal fate? And above all what about the wicked and the tyrannical who prayed just as I did? Would they be gaining more and more power to improve and enlarge their evil nature and designs? What educational or moral lessons could be drawn from the descriptions of battles between goddesses and demons of different shapes and nomenclatures where the result was a foregone conclusion? Why stretch a simple truth in such imaginary detail and unnecessary gory length?

Recitation of the *Ram Charit Manas*, though, did induce some good morals and habits. And the Gita was certainly a different matter altogether, for every fresh reading brought out a new meaning of life and a new dimension of spirituality. Why not then read each verse of the Gita with greater concentration and deeper insight, rather than spend time in other formalities and rituals?

These and many other questions and doubts would come to my mind repeatedly and I felt guilty that my dedication was not complete or single-minded, and that I was at heart a non-believer. I could not discuss these things with anybody. There was no understanding or impartial soul around. Moreover, I wanted to spread the impression of being a devout, surrendering type of religious person and the exposition of these doubts would have marred that image.

In this motley daily worship the question of utility was always haunting my mind. Were the modern merry-makers right when they said that we were only beguiling ourselves in this exercise? Could this sort of prayer or worship be gainfully exchanged for some more result-oriented activity? If all this worship was really for progress in career and prosperity, why not just spend more time in preparing for some professional competitive examinations that would open doors for better government jobs and more money? Nevertheless, despite this confusion, somewhere deep down I was also praying for some meaning, for some direct achievement in the inner world of my mind.

On one such *Navratra*, perhaps in the month of October in 1958, I was once again busy in my usual six-hourly assorted ritualistic worship, but more than ever my inner being thirsted for some deeper meaning, so that I might continue my practice with confidence and conviction. Then, on the seventh day, while I was reciting the thirteenth chapter of the Gita, its meaning seemed to emerge vividly and visually from its lines and letters.

'Know that I am the one and only knower in all fields'.

As I read these lines, the knower within me became 'me' in a mysterious manner, and instead of being the reader, I became the knower. I was lost in a higher state of consciousness. My 'me' became Krishna, the all-knowing entity. I cannot describe that experience in words. It was the first time in my life that I had a glimpse of my innermost self.

So far, my knowing meant identification with the 'object known' and this process was my normal way of knowing everything. For the first time I became the knower and saw him in me (or me in him). It was an all-encompassing knower-known consciousness. I became a witness and my awareness became distinct from my sensory knowledge.

In other words, the knowing entity is distinct from knowledge and is the same in all beings. The implications of this realisation are soul-stirring and deep. Normally it is very difficult to separate the knower from the knowledge. Although in essence it is the knower who becomes knowledge, yet one is a 'doer' and the other is a 'done'. The subject, the nucleus, can be felt separately from the process and the result of the act of knowing. This is a most subtle psychic exercise. It requires a realisation of the existence of another entity which is above the knower and the knowledge both. He is called *purushottam* in the Gita and is understood as the witnessing entity.

In spiritual philosophy this is the 'supra-subjective' and can be clearly realized or understood only by the grace of the guru or the all-knowing entity. The experience of this realization suddenly transforms the entire being, as it is quite different from any other experience or 'becoming'. This layer of being reveals itself miraculously during the process of *sadhana* (meditation and spiritual practice) and cannot be attained directly. In fact, an effort to repeat this experience is what is called *smaran* or recollection in spiritual terms. But recollection is only possible after the basic or first revelation, which is almost effortless. When one is making an effort, one cannot feel or know oneself, because the knower is busy in 'doing' and cannot experience its own 'being'.

The dawn of this revelation about the 'self' is sudden and happens like lightning. The first glimpse is full of so many pleasant psychic and physical sensations that the knower becomes vibrated with bliss. This bliss is distinctly superior and quite separate from the sensation of pleasure.

The death of a desire through its fulfilment normally gives us a feeling of temporary respite until another desire takes hold of us. For instance, we are thirsty and seek water. When water is found and taken, the projection of the mind which is called 'thirst' merges in the original mental stuff and we feel some kind of relief which is called pleasure. This pleasure is the reverse of the pain which 'thirst' was causing us. Removal of the feeling of thirst causes relief.

But the feeling of bliss is not caused by removal of one desire, it is in a way caused by the destruction of the very cause which creates desires again and again in us. It is the reverse or obverse of our normal existence, which consists of innumerable births and deaths of desires in a continuous flux. Bliss can be called another level of being, or super-consciousness.

So when I understood the full meaning of the verse 'Know that the knower in all bodies is one and the same and it is Me' it was like awakening to a new reality. I realised that Lord Krishna is making knowledge possible in all living beings. My normal ego, the small 'I', was lost in the ocean of the super-ego which unites all in one. It suddenly struck me that wherever there is life and mind, wherever there is the 'I' feeling, it is universally one and the same entity.

As this dawned upon me, I began to experience immeasurable light points raining over my body. The burden of existence was suddenly lifted from me and I became weightless. All the cells of my brain began to readjust, to make a different 'I'. I read the verse again and again and a sensation of coolness, freshness and happiness swept over my whole frame. For the first time I had a glimpse into myself. Normally I existed as knowledge, the knower being hidden, unseen in the knowledge. Now I was looking at the origin of knowledge and I was distinctly different from it.

The meaning of the scriptures, wherein God is explained as all-pervading and all-knowing, became clearer and nearer. Krishna says: 'I am the innermost entity in every heart, and all memory, knowledge and forgetfulness is due to Me'. These psychic processes within me, then, are also Krishna himself working as 'I' in me. And I am a part of him — working from this body. How close the Lord is! To find Krishna so personal and near was intoxicating.

When I got up from my *puja* it was a different 'I'. But as soon as I began to interact with others and work in the home and office, I lapsed into my former self, so that this experience remained only a pleasant memory.

How I wish, perhaps presumptuously, that I could have stabilized into this new discovery of the self by remaining immovable for days together like the Buddha.

In search of a guru on my way to Neelkanth at Badrinath. From top left to bottom right: my uncle, myself, our driver, my sons Mukt and Gagan, and my wife Sarla

In simple terms, what we have to do is to return home from where we came. We have all come from the Supreme Entity, the Nucleus of the universe. We have to return to the same destination... When one is tired of this world and worldliness, one yearns to go back to spirituality — one's home. And what is our permanent abode, our home? The Supreme Consciousness. Spiritual practice (sadhana), therefore, is the process of returning home. It is a simple task. It requires no scholarship, no knowledge, no intellectual faculty, no long and tedious lecturing.

28 May 1967, Allahabad

Initiation

Entering the scene of the Indian Administrative Service (IAS), after nearly five years of academic career as a college lecturer in English Literature, was a sea change in my life. I was in the corridors of power and pelf.

The officers I was around lived in the spacious bungalows of secluded government colonies and enjoyed their drinks and night-life full of parties and frolics. I was shocked by this very different way of life and I found myself at a crossing — on the one hand a life of power and of 'eat, drink and be merry', and on the other, a life of spiritual searching and inward journey.

Soon after joining my posting in the Indian Administrative Service, I decided to go on a pilgrimage to the Himalayan shrines in search of a real guru. It took about two months, traversing on foot from Rishikesh to Jyotirmath, Badrinath and Kedarnath. I stayed in wayside inns after every five or six kilometres and enquired about the ashrams or caves where saints lived and did their penances. I met many saints during this time, some practising Hath yoga, others doing Raj yoga, some living in caves and keeping a burning *dhuni* alive, others in their loincloth and with their long matted hair. I questioned them about the spiritual path, but was neither satisfied with their replies nor with their way of life. I came back disappointed. I was on the verge of giving up, but then came a messenger from my would-be guru.

At the time I was Deputy Secretary of Finance in the Government of Rajasthan and was distributing grants-in-aid to voluntary organisations running their own schools and colleges. I used to read their applications, interview them and determine the amount of aid to be given. On one such occasion of conducting interviews, I received a note that a certain Acharya Lallan was waiting to meet me. I thought he must be from some Sanskrit school or college, as traditional Sanskrit teachers often prefixed their names with the 'Acharya' title. When I called him in, I saw that he was a young bearded man clad completely in white and quite an impressive figure.

'Acharyaji, what can I do for you? What are you managing or running?' I asked.

'I am not managing anything, nor am I running anything. I came to discuss philosophy with you', he replied.

Quite surprised at this unexpected request, I told him I was a little tired from the day's work and that my office was not an appropriate place for such a discussion. But, I added, he was most welcome to come to my house after dinner; I would invite a few of my friends and we could discuss philosophy to our heart's content. He agreed, and at around nine o'clock that same evening Acharya Lallan joined our little gathering on the lawn outside my house.

There were four or five of us. My neighbour, Vinod Chand Pandey, who later became the Cabinet Secretary of India, had joined us together with his elder brother, Govind Chand Pandey, Vice-chancellor of the Rajasthan University.

Acharya Lallan then gave a talk on *sanchar* and *pratisanchar*, in which he described how creation began and how from this creation one can return to the creator. Though it was a short talk it had a deep impact on our minds. None of us had ever heard or studied the ideas Acharya Lallan offered. We began to question him. We questioned him on the traditional concepts of *jap* (recitation) and idol worship and many other things, and by the end of it we were thoroughly impressed by this man who gave us a new perspective on very old and traditional concepts.

We invited him to come again the following day. This question-and-answer session too was very satisfying. His explanations were not mere verbology, but logic and faith and mystery all rolled into one. Finally, Acharya Lallan said: 'It is a deep philosophy and it will take us days to discuss, but why don't you take initiation and start your journey towards the search for truth?' We all agreed.

Acharya Lallan invited my wife and I to meet him at five o'clock the next morning. We took our time and arrived at around six thirty instead, thinking that after all we should be at ease during the time of initiation. But he said that as we had not come on time he could not initiate us that day and we should return at the correct time the following day. We were a little taken aback that this man, who seemed so pleasant and simple, had become so strict. However, we were curious and felt that there must be something very valuable that he wanted to give us, albeit on his own terms. The next day we arrived at his place on time and were initiated.

That was the beginning of my journey on this path I am treading till today. But it was just that, a beginning. I continued some of my earlier rituals and my wife continued to worship the picture of Shiva. We both added the new mantra given by Acharya Lallan to our practices like a footnote.

What is Guru? The Samskrta word 'Guru' has two parts. It is a compound word. 'Gu' means darkness. 'Ru' means dispelling entity. The one who dispels is called 'Ru'. Guru means the entity who dispels darkness from the mind.

17 August 1979, Taipei

Jamalpur

Jamalpur is a small and sleepy town in south Bihar. But it has had a big and awakening influence on my life. It was here that I met my master for the first time some forty-five years ago. That meeting changed the entire course of my life and filled me with the meaning and joy of existence. Not only did the aim and object of life become clear for the first time, but my very raw and sketchy knowledge about the Indian scriptures and philosophy also acquired some ripening and certitude. All this has been so becalming and restful for my mind. My direction became more definite and my efforts more systematic.

I first came to Jamalpur in the summer of 1962 while I was on my way to Puri (a Hindu pilgrimage place on the east coast of India), where I wanted to spend my earned leave of more than a month or so. Jamalpur was a small detour and an adjustment of only two or three days, to which I was persuaded by Acarya Satyanandaji Avadhuta, the first *sanyasi* (monk) of Ananda Marga. Throughout my childhood and early years as an adult I have had a lot of curiosity to meet spiritual personages. For this purpose I had travelled far and wide and met many famous names of the time, as well as lesser known yogis who lived in the caves and ashrams of the Himalayas. I had also been initiated into the practice of Ananda Marga meditation about six months back, but had not progressed much due to my own lethargy and lack of full faith and sincerity.

After a journey full of misadventures and inconveniences, I reached Jamalpur station on a burning midday of May. On inquiring about the location of the Ananda Marga ashram from taxi drivers, rickshaw pullers and coolies, I came to realize that Ananda Marga was almost an unknown commodity in its birthplace.

This was perhaps one of several 'wake-up calls' or surprises I had as I was getting to know and understand Ananda Marga.

As regards misadventure on the way to Jamalpur, I had disembarked on the platform of Agra station to buy some fruits. While I was haggling for their price, my train, the Toofan Mail, steamed off. I ran to catch the speeding train, spilled the fruits and lost my slippers on the platform. With great difficulty, I secured a foothold on a hot doorstep on one of the last compartments, which was securely closed from the inside. I started hanging by the red-hot handle of the door while the train gathered more and more speed. Both the foothold and the handle were so hot that I did not expect to survive till the next halt, which was to be between one and a half to two hours away. I felt miserable and began to curse the day I accepted the suggestion of Dada Satyanandaji to visit my new guru. At this thought, suddenly the train made an unscheduled halt at the next wayside station, and with a huge sigh of relief, I ran and entered my compartment in a distraught, dishevelled and tired condition.

The incident, as strange as it was, was perhaps a kind of shock treatment to put my mind in a more receptive posture for catching subtler vibrations. Other small incidents happened which, in retrospect I feel, were also meant to disturb the placid and static state of my mind. Unless we dig the land, no seed can be sown. *Tantra* (the path of spiritual liberation), in particular, is nothing but a series of shake-ups of varying intensity to awaken the mind to the divinity within.

Anyway, when I reached the Jamalpur ashram in 1962 it was a monumental disappointment. The ashram was situated on a narrow dirty and winding street, and contrary to normal expectations, the place and its surroundings were dry and desolate. There were hardly two or three rooms, which had not been completed yet, with dusty floors and open spaces in between. And on top of it all, there was no sign of festivity here. Not a soul to inform the traveller which way to go and where and how.

My wife and I were in dire need of a long cool bath and some rest, preferably beneath some lush green, shady trees or on a turf that had been profusely watered in the morning. Instead, we had to return disappointed to the hot and crowded station, while the midday sun of summer was pouring fire on the burning earth all around.

Here was another crucial psychological moment when we nearly decided to catch the next train to anywhere to escape this inferno. A very weak, almost casual help meanwhile arrived in the form of some information that the Ananda Marga function we were seeking here in Jamalpur was being held at Munger instead, some half an hour's taxi-drive away on the banks of the Ganges. My wife and I reluctantly accepted the option of adding another half an hour's ordeal to our travel troubles, if only to give a piece of our mind to the person who had extended the invitation and put us through all this hassle unnecessarily.

So we reached a big *dharamshala* (traveller's lodge) in Munger, which was bustling with people and preparations for some important event. Our first necessity on reaching there was a hearty bath. We dumped our luggage in one corner of a common room and hired a cycle rickshaw to take us to a ghat on the Ganges. On the way to the Ganges, we quenched our thirst and hunger with big, iced glasses of *lassi*, while the rickshaw puller was humming some sweet unfamiliar song in what appeared to be his native tongue. The waters of the Ganges were refreshingly cool, as if Gangotri, the source of the Ganges River, was only a few miles upstream and not thousands of dusty miles away. We prolonged our bath to wash away all the heat, sweat and anguish.

Our rickshaw puller waited patiently all the while. When he had taken us back to the *dharamshala*, I discovered that there was no change in my purse. I, therefore, requested him to wait while I brought the change from the room within. But to my utter surprise, when in a few minutes I returned, I discovered that the man had gone. I inquired from a number of rickshaw pullers standing near the *dharamshala* about this man, who was tall, well built, dark complexioned and had a slightly philosophical look. No one seemed to know him. Later on however, some senior devotees told me that the description I gave for the rickshaw puller fitted Kalikanandaji, one of Baba's first disciples, who lives a saintly life incognito, and now and then comes to help new spiritual aspirants, particularly when and where Baba was around.

In the evening the main spiritual discourse by Baba took place in the open courtyard of the *dharamshala*. I secured for myself a vantage position in the front row and waited for the arrival of the guru. As soon as Baba arrived it was as if the entire place transformed into a madhouse. Some started crying, others laughing, still others were spreading themselves and throwing their hands and feet together, some shaking violently and making strange sounds and a couple almost fainting in ecstasy.

I had never seen anything like this before despite having attended numerous spiritual congregations. I witnessed these scenes in utter bewilderment. Baba started speaking but I was hardly listening to what he was saying.

My attention was completely distracted by what was happening around me. People continued to express themselves in a most unusual manner during the entire discourse.

When we returned to our lodge after the discourse, my wife and I exchanged notes on the evening's experiences and both felt uneasy and perturbed about what had transpired before us. What surprised me most was that, while introducing myself to people sitting beside me in the gathering, I had found that some of them were high-ranked officers in the civil services. They seemed to be quite respectable people and it was difficult to imagine that all these people were fakes, planted in the congregation to dramatise the whole phenomenon.

So I decided to meet some of these people and find out more about our curious experience. Many of the officers were staying at the Circuit House, a government-owned guest house where senior civil servants were allowed to stay on visits.

The first person I met there was Mr Prasad, a senior officer in the Indian Customs and Central Excise Service. I asked him why he was weeping when he saw Baba. 'Don't bother', he replied, 'you will also weep one day'. This was no explanation. So I met another officer from the Indian Police Service, Mr Akhori, and inquired about the reason for his abnormal screaming and shaking of limbs. He said that these were simply expressions of devotion. I questioned other officers as well and they all assured me that what I had seen was a normal reaction to every Baba *darshan* (an instance of being in his presence).

The puzzling experience of that evening had become more intriguing after speaking to these people and I decided that instead of just one day's stay in Jamalpur as originally planned, I would now extend our visit for a few more days to get to the bottom of this mystery of the Baba *darshan*. So we returned to Jamalpur and were offered a place at one of Baba's ardent devotees, Acharya Bindeshwariji's house, where we received excellent hospitality.

Every day I would go to the ashram and listen to Baba, who spoke not just on spiritual philosophy, but on a range of subjects including geography, linguistics, history and economics. It was such a mixed fare and his insights and depth of knowledge were so fascinating that I began to love his talks.

In the evenings Baba used to go for a walk in the nearby fields and sit with his disciples for some time on a rectangular tomb before returning home. According to the local history, a brave British soldier and a tiger once fought fiercely in those fields and both succumbed to their injuries from the encounter. To honour their bravery and commemorate that incident, people from the area buried the soldier and the tiger not far from each other in two sections of the field. Baba usually sat on the tiger's grave. Four disciples could accompany him during each walk. I was eager for this opportunity and did not have to wait long.

He makes you do sadhana, furnishes you with intellect and strength — surrender yourself to His will. Off with your load of self-conceit. Lighten the burden of your life and let yourself drift on the course of His will. It is He who is teaching you sadhana in the guise of a Guru. You are plundering His mercy through everything day and night. Go on working selflessly like a machine, leaving the doership to Him. How little can your small intellect comprehend His inscrutable liila! How little can it be analysed! So, instead of analysing His liila, only keep the bearing of that inscrutable juggler ever aglow before your eyes.

1956, Bhagalpur

Field Walk

It was a very hot and sultry summer evening when I got my first chance to go for a field walk with Baba.

I had heard a lot about his great spiritual powers. I had witnessed nearly one-third of a big gathering consisting of men and women of all ages and from all parts of India going into ecstasy by his mere presence. My host in Jamalpur, Acharya Bindeshwariji, had also been wonder-struck. He would become most abnormal in the presence of Baba and had the power to give others a brief taste of higher states of consciousness by just a touch or exhortation. Very rational people occupying high-ranking positions in government service considered Baba equivalent to Shiva or Krishna. While I was in the ashram, I heard people relating their occult experiences that they attributed to their practice of Ananda Marga meditation. Some told of how, as a result of Baba's teachings, they broke with the caste system and were met with fierce opposition. But, by his divine grace, their adversaries grudgingly came to respect their universal outlook. And above all, I had myself experienced Baba's gigantic intellectual heights while listening to his informal discourses in the small room of the Jamalpur ashram.

Self-conscious as I was, I debated at length in my mind all the alternatives of dress and demeanour I should adopt for that special evening. Should I be in the semi-formal dress of trousers and shirt or in Indian casuals like *kurta-pyjama*? I used to perspire a lot in this sort of weather and my perspiration was most stinking. So should I use perfume or powder or body spray to avoid the stink emitting from me? Perfume would be too loud and ostentatious. Body powder may get wet soon and become uncomfortable and I had no proper body spray with me.

And when I was with Baba, should I walk ahead, behind or side by side with him? Walking in front would be audacious, walking in step would be a bit embarrassing and walking behind may not be convenient for conversation.

And finally, while with Baba, should I break the ice first and start a conversation by asking some question or should I wait until he speaks to me? And if I was to begin, what kind of questions should I put to him? We had all been told that the field walk was part of Baba's rest time and he should not be bothered with serious questions or philosophical discussions.

Even after long deliberations on each of the above and many other matters, I remained completely confused and undecided about my options. There were three more people going on this field walk, but there was no occasion to consult them.

The time to reach the appointed triangular green spot, a little away from Baba's modest railway quarters, came sooner than expected and after a quick bath, I was there along with three other gentlemen, whom I did not know at all. Everyone appeared somewhat nervous and anxious and it seemed that their heads were also full of internal debates. None of us exchanged our introductions or spoke much before Baba's arrival. He was clad in a white *kurta* and *dhoti* and was smiling and munching on something. He immediately put us all at ease as each of us prostrated before him and introduced ourselves to him.

We passed through the narrow and noisy lanes of the town in deep silence until we crossed the railway over-bridge and reached the border of a famous field in that town. It lay adjacent to a lake and was partially skirted by wooded hills and a deep valley, called the Death Valley, perhaps, due to the wild beasts that used to live there. In the dusk of that evening, the field looked like a vast shoreless ocean, a pathless green expanse, which served as a perfect venue for our mysterious occult experiences.

Our field walk began almost imperceptibly with Baba walking briskly and slightly ahead, the four of us trailing close behind him. Soon I forgot all about my companions and became totally absorbed in Baba's figure, which looked like a bright white phantom walking on the dark green grass. I could see the twitching movement of one or two of his fingers. He had joined his palms behind his back and was walking with his chest outstretched, head held high in front.

Without making a conscious effort, I began to pray in my mind, repeating again and again that he may take me in his shelter and give me all that is best and highest in this world. I became so absorbed in these mental prayers that I even lost sight of him.

Suddenly, Baba turned softly towards me and said, 'No prayers'.

This awakened me to him and the walk. The realization struck my mind like a lightning bolt; he is not only with me, but in me. He knows what I am thinking. It gave me a pleasant sort of thrill and shock.

As it dawned on me that Baba could see what was going on in my mind, I was full of awe and praise for him. Early in my life, I had learnt many hymns of praise for gods and goddesses and quite involuntarily some of them began to surface in my mind. I began to praise him through the internal recital of some of these hymns.

'You are the greatest of the deities, the whole universe exists at your pleasure, the sun and the moon and the rain and the wind are all your obedient servants' and so on I thought. As I took pleasure in repeating one hymn after another, I again became oblivious of the proximity of Baba walking with me in person.

Then, again he leaned towards me and said softly, 'No *stuti* (praise), no not this'.

Another shock. He did not like this attitude of my mind either. Supplicant or servile were both wrong attitudes towards the Lord. However, I was not aware of any third attitude. Therefore, almost in a semi-resentful mood I adopted the yogic attitude, as I knew it to be at that time, namely, to stop all thoughts and keep the mind forcefully vacant. So I strained to remain like a piece of wood, not allowing any perception, imagination, feeling or thought to arise and fill my mind.

Baba now faced me and told me that this was an unnatural state and I could not stay in it for long. 'No pressure on the mind', he said. 'You cannot stop the vibrations of an active mind for long'.

By now I had exhausted all options and could think of nothing else but to surrender myself completely to the great person who had given me full freedom, and with that freedom he had so far given corrections in attitude as well.

I said to myself: 'Lord, I know only this, that you are great and want to lead me to the most beneficial and correct path. But I have tried all that I was familiar with and now I know not what to do. So I surrender myself to you. I cannot devise what is the best as far as my approach to you is concerned. So lead me on where you want. I am yours. I give up making any more foolish attempts. In fact I have no other course left'.

As I was elaborating these ideas, Baba put one of his arms around my waist and told me to look ahead towards a rectangular tomb. This was the tiger's grave, our destination for the walk. We had come so close to it and I was not even aware of it.

I felt elated and blissful. He had touched me, taken me into his care; all my confusions were over. I no longer required exerting myself on the question of what was good and what was bad, whither to go and how to walk. The period of my trial and error was over. It seemed that he was there in my mind all along with every vibration, watching and guiding my 'self' from within, though unbeknownst to me. I heaved a sigh of relief only when I gave up and he took over.

Now this was going to be my correct attitude of mind, both in my *sadhana* and in my thoughts and actions. My own vision was limited and my initiatives were restricted by my past experiences. And here I was on entirely new ground, walking with the all-knowing, all-powerful Almighty himself. Here I had to let myself go. He was the player and I was but a tool. How all stress and strain, all ifs and buts, all pros and cons subsided in his presence, in the lap of the one who was the object of my goal and search.

Later on, I realized that he was playing the same game with all four of us. And now

I feel that he is busy in playing this *liila*, this cosmic game, with the entire expressed universe. Egos big and small strut and fret foolishly and boast of achieving this and that. Spiritual aspirants adopt a hundred paths to attain him. Some only pray, others praise and pray and still others practice yoga and *tantra* to attain him. There is nothing wrong in all this. But once he reveals himself to us, when he is before us, it is no use doing all this for him. The best thing is to give up and sit in his lap, to let things happen and recognise them as his eternal play, and enjoy.

One person is scholarly, another is rich;
but they may or may not be devotees.
The only thing that the devotee needs is love
for the Lord. When all feelings, all attachments,
are directed towards Him, then it is devotion.
The only qualification is a sincere heart.
If your heart is pure, you need nothing else.

22 January 1971, Ranchi

Shiva Darshan

After hearing Baba speak, after my personal contact with him and my subsequent field walks in his uplifting and inspiring company, I had fully accepted him as my guru. However, my wife, Sarla, remained suspicious and even frightened of associating herself with Baba and his followers.

She resented my decision to postpone our trip to Puri after the theatrical and eccentric behaviour of the people we had seen in Baba's presence at Munger. There was some black magic going on, she felt, and staying any longer in the company of Baba's disciples would surely have an adverse impact on our mental condition. It did not help that we were staying with Acharya Bindeshwariji, who was an embodiment of strange outbursts of ostensibly devotional expressions.

Ever since she was initiated into Ananda Marga's spiritual practice, Sarla complained sometimes of seeing a dark human shadow emerging from Shiva's picture, which she had continued to worship along with doing her meditation. This shadow would move intimidatingly towards the ceiling causing fear in her mind. On other occasions, she saw a beam of light of unusual brilliance emerge from the picture and engulf the room, filling her with a kind of sudden exhilaration.

When she narrated these visions to me, I ridiculed her and deemed them to be a figment of her imagination. She would sometimes discontinue the new additions to her prayer, the mental repetition of her spiritual mantra, but felt more restless thereafter. Her meditation continued in fits and starts.

Ananda Marga had thus far been an unsettling experience for Sarla. Her dissatisfaction in Jamalpur was mounting, as every day I would join the other men who gathered in the small room and enjoyed Baba's discourse while the ladies had to sit outside on the verandah. Many a time they could not even hear what was going on in the room. Sarla found it quite boring to sit at the gate and witness the blissful expressions on the faces of those who were gathered within the room, and after one or two visits she stopped accompanying me to the ashram.

It needs mentioning here that Baba's room in Jamalpur was very small for the number of visitors who used to gather there. The men were already pressed shoulder-to-shoulder, toe-to-toe. It would have been socially unacceptable, given the mores of the traditional Hindu society, to have both men and women squeezed together into that small space.

Anyhow, each day when I returned to Bindeshwariji's house after spending time with Baba, I would have to face my upset wife imploring me to set off for Puri as soon as possible. After a few days I gave in and booked tickets for our onward travel to Puri on the coming Sunday. On that Sunday afternoon, I requested her to come with me to see Baba one last time and she agreed.

We were travelling in a rickshaw and as we arrived at the ashram we saw Baba coming from his house via a short-cut through a broken boundary wall. I asked Sarla to take this rare opportunity to meet and greet Baba in person while I settled the fare with the rickshaw-puller. By the time I was finished haggling, I saw that Baba had taken Sarla under his umbrella and they had already entered the ashram.

I hurried behind Baba to secure a place, barely catching a glimpse of Sarla who was sitting outside his room as usual. Baba's discourse that day was on a difficult philosophical subject and the talk was rather long. Throughout the talk I was fretting that Sarla would be getting impatient and must be really cross with me for putting her through this boredom again.

When Baba had left, I walked towards Sarla nervously, ready to suffer a dressing down. She was leaning against a wall with her eyes closed. Tears slipped from beneath her eyelids. But to my surprise, her face bore an expression of deep content. She did not immediately respond when I called her nor when I placed my hand on her shoulder. Only after a couple of minutes did she gradually open her eyes still full of tears. I told her softly that we should leave now as our train was departing in two hours or so. 'No', she said, 'we are not going anywhere'. She expressed her wish to stay for at least one more week in Baba's company. I was at a complete loss as to what had caused this reversal in her attitude.

Later, as we were returning to Bindeshwariji's house, she told me that as she touched Baba's feet in salutation, she had tasted a divine ecstasy and that she now understood why devotees expressed themselves so abnormally on seeing him. As she was immersed in this blissful state of mind, she felt as if all her confusions were swept away and she now wanted nothing more than to be here with Baba.

The next day was a Monday — a half fast day for Sarla, according to her traditional practices of Shiva worship. She came to the ashram somewhat early and began to look for flowers to make a garland for the worship of

Lord Shiva. She could only find blossoms of the wild *aak* which was growing abundantly on the broken mud wall that formed the outer boundary of the ashram. Having gathered quite a few, she weaved them into a small garland to be taken to some Shiva temple. Meanwhile Baba arrived and everyone rushed towards his room, for in the mornings he would stay there for only a very short time, before proceeding to his office for work.

As usual, Sarla sat near the entrance to the room looking steadily at Baba. Every day, someone used to bring a garland for Baba, but on that day no one had brought any, or perhaps, the person who brought it regularly had not come. As Baba sat down, everyone was waiting for the garland, but there was none. Then, as if in a trance, Sarla got up, walked into the room and offered her small garland to Baba.

Baba gave one of his soft divine smiles and said, 'Oh mother! You have made me Sadashiva!' Sarla looked a bit stunned and could only withdraw with difficulty from the room.

A few minutes after Baba had left I found her outside yet again lost in some sort of trance. She later told me that as Baba was uttering those words, his figure transformed in her vision, into that of Lord Shiva and then he became a ball of effulgence, sweet and blissful. She sat immersed in that glorious vision and got a deeper taste of the nectar she had savoured the day before.

We stayed on in the blistering heat of Jamalpur to witness the wonderful spiritual phenomenon that was my guru. We became attached to the small room where Baba used to meet his disciples morning and evening, to the field and the tiger's grave and to the hills, dales and lakes of Jamalpur and above all to the whole atmosphere of that place, where every day we received new experiences, more spiritual knowledge, more divine love and more and more of that subtle sweetness, which used to permeate our whole being there.

Now whom should you take to be your ideal? …
Your ideal has to be perfect — so your ideal
is to be the Lord and the Lord alone.
No one else should be your ideal. And you should
not pray to the Lord, 'Make me this, make me
that; make me Arjuna or make me Sudama'.
No, such should never be your prayer,
for suppose the Lord wants you to become even
greater than what you are praying to become?
In such a case, you are creating a hindrance
to your own welfare.

March 1963, Jamalpur

The Ideal

Was the blissful experience that I had while reading the Gita during one of my *Navratra pujas* genuine or just a figment of my imagination? During my first visit to Jamalpur, many a time this question came to my mind while I was listening to Baba's discourses in the ashram. But I never had the courage or opportunity to talk to Baba about it. Even before then, whenever I had gone to a saint or spiritual person, I hoped they might speak of my realization. I had gone to dozens of such eminent and famous people but none answered my internal question.

Gradually, I had almost forgotten the experience. Then one morning it so transpired that I was alone with Baba for a few minutes, while Dada Abhedanandji, Baba's then PA, was busy with some preparation outside. I did *sashtanga pranam* (prostration) and sat quietly at Baba's feet. Quite unexpectedly and without any context, Baba asked me, 'So you have known the Ideal?'

I was speechless at first, but then I realized that his question was in reference to my revelation during that *Navratra* while reading the Gita.

'Baba, I do not know what it was. You alone know!' I replied.

Baba smiled and said, 'You have known the Ideal. Now waste no time and pursue it'.

So this was an important personal guidance I received from Baba on my spiritual path. The next guidance I received one evening while walking with him in the quiet solitude of the holy fields of Jamalpur. In these evening group walks, Baba would explain a thousand things to us. But the essence of all his talks was self-realization and social progress. Each evening while walking with him, I was silently praying that he may lead me to the goal of life.

On one of these cool summer evenings, he took me aside from the rest of the group and began to explain to me the history of the hills and mountains that were visible from the field. We were walking and talking. There was a half moon in the clear sky. The green fields, the skirting hills and the faint moonlit night made a splendid atmosphere for him to enter my psyche. I was overjoyed to find him so close and alone with me.

After explaining the geography of the area, he transported me to historical scenes, as he described the distant kingdom of Mahabharata and the sages travelling through the dense forests of the surrounding chain of mountains running East to Northwest.

It suddenly dawned on me that lord Krishna himself was explaining all these phenomena. How else could he know all this and in such detail? I fell at his feet in the grass and he gently told me to rise and stand. As I was regaining awareness of the present, he assured me, 'Your work has been done!'

I knew then that I was in his charge and that he was the guardian angel always present in my mind, as a witness and as one who controls and creates all movement.

After that first fateful meeting in the summer of 1962, I continued to visit Jamalpur as many times as possible, with or without any obvious excuse or pretext. It became a Mecca for me and my family. My brothers and sons too became part of Baba's charmed circle. Each member of my family had their own experiences that bound them to him. In fact, since that first visit, the main topic in all our family gatherings or personal conversations has more often than not been Baba. Such is the sweet embalmed existence of his love that even after these forty-six years, the one and only staple pabulum of my mental being continues to be him.

When one is ensconced in the exalted state due to the grace of Guru, what stage does one's intuition reach? What sort of realization does one attain? One discovers the divine play of the Infinite Entity in each and every finite manifestation. One realizes that the Infinite Entity who is ever-present in His vast Cosmic stance is also ever-present in every molecule and atom. One experiences that the entire universe is vibrated and invigorated with His unending Cosmic flow. Every entity of this universe, big and small, every minute expression of pain and pleasure of the numerous microcosms lies within His vast Ocean of Cosmic Bliss.

11 November 1957, Nathnagar

Neem Karoli Baba

It was the summer of 1962 and my wife and I were returning from Jamalpur after about a month away from home. Due to the many changes and delays in our travel plans during this trip, we could no longer use our originally made travel reservations and had to settle for places available in a third class sleeper coach.

In those days a journey in a third class sleeper coach was like traversing a street in hell. A child would urinate from the top berth drenching all on the middle and lower berths. The compartment was full of the smoke of cigarettes. The old and the sick would cough interminably and after their marathon bouts of coughing, they would ease themselves over the edge of their berths and spit from wherever they were sitting or sleeping. Loud talk and hot discussions would go on between passengers throughout the night. And instead of protecting the compartment from travellers without tickets or reservations, the ticket checker would allow such passengers into the compartments for a small monetary compensation, giving them any vacant spaces between the berths to sleep. One could not walk to the toilet without offending these intruders. It was a crowded world of filth, smoke and noise.

Despite all this, our minds were so much soaked in the peace and beatitude of Jamalpur that we floated effortlessly above these inconveniences. My nostrils were filled with a divine fragrance and I had the feeling that Baba was always near. Nothing could disturb me from that heavenly bliss in which I had lived for nearly a month. My wife was similarly immune to the disturbing surroundings of our train journey and slept sweetly and soundly throughout the stinking and deafening din.

We reached Delhi in this immunised embalmed mood and drove straight to the Constitution Club, a spacious building in

New Delhi where officers of the Indian Administrative Service could stay if they were not allotted permanent residences. My close friend, Vinod Pandey, lived there in an apartment, and we became his guests.

Before leaving Jamalpur, on my last field walk with Baba, he had enquired about the well-being of my eldest son, Anand, as we sat together on the tiger's grave. 'Anand does not know that I know him', Baba had said.

I was surprised by his enquiry, for I had never given details of my children nor their names to Baba. I replied that we had left Anand with relatives in my home town of Kota, and that he must be doing fine. But Baba's question had left some concern in my mind.

So as soon as we reached Delhi, I picked up the phone and rang up Kota to hear how Anand was doing. He had gone to the railway station to get the local newspaper, wherein his twelfth class results were published. The newspaper used to come from Delhi to Kota by midnight in parcels. I was relieved to know later that all was well with him and that he had passed his exams with flying colours.

My wife and I were quite tired from our journey, and after taking a bath and an early supper wanted to go to bed. But this was not to be, as our host requested that I go with him to meet a famous saint, who was staying nearby in the quarter of a Joint Secretary of the Government of India. After meeting Baba I no longer had any special desire to see anyone else for spiritual guidance.

Anyway, when Vinod and I reached the aforementioned house at around nine o'clock, there was a sea of cars at the gate and it appeared that all who mattered in the government in Delhi had assembled there that night. We parked our car a little distance away from the house and walked to meet the saint. We reached the front door of the spacious house and made our way to the drawing room where the gathering was being held. I half opened the door of the hall to see that the room was already overcrowded and there wasn't enough space for even a child to squeeze in the back row of the gathering. On a wooden cot was sitting a huge frame clad only in a *lungi*. It was Neem Karoli Baba, a famous *tantrik* and saint well known all over India, and particularly so in the state of Uttar Pradesh. He was sitting at the other end of the room facing the crowd and the door through which we peeped. After surveying the scene for about two or three minutes, Vinod and I agreed that there was no way to push in, and we began to make our way back towards the car to return home.

But we must have walked only a few steps when a man came running after us from the hall. He told us that Neem Karoli Baba had seen us when we opened the door and he wanted us to come in. With some surprise, we returned to the hall. The crowd made way for us and we were taken to the wooden dais on which Neem Karoli Baba sat. He looked at me intensely and asked all those sitting inside to vacate the room for some time. In a few minutes the crowd withdrew. Then he requested Vinod to withdraw as well.

Now Neem Karoli Baba and I were the only two in the room. He beckoned me to sit near him and asked me whether I had met my guru. I replied in the affirmative. He then wanted to know which lesson I was practising. I answered accordingly. He caressed me lovingly and put his hand on my head.

'You are blessed that you have met Guruji and that he has bestowed so much love on you', he said.

I listened to him with great surprise. He then asked me not to give up my *sadhana* nor my guru and once again called me very fortunate. Thereafter I was allowed to leave and everyone else was called back into the hall.

This miraculous confirmation of Baba's greatness filled me with immense joy. When I related the whole conversation to Vinod he told me more about Neem Karoli Baba's incredible powers. Thus, I was further elated to know that these reassuring words came from such a great saint. That night my sleep was filled with spiritual dreams.

The next day my wife and I continued our journey home to Jaipur.

The lyres of all minds play
to the same tune today.
There is fragrance in all hearts.
You came onto this earth
with Your exquisite appearance
and gave the same feeling to all.
Do not tear my garland of flowers,
my entire wealth of compassion.
Come close to me,
come closer, still closer,
take all that I have.

18 September 1982
Prabhat Sangeet Nr. 4

Kota

Kota is a small city on the banks of the ancient and perennial river named Charmanavati or Chambal. It was the capital of an erstwhile princely state of Rajasthan. I adopted Kota as my home in 1942 when I came there for my college education. Many of my relatives still live there today.

On my return from Jamalpur in 1962 I stayed in Kota for a couple of days before continuing on to Jaipur. Limited time permitted me to meet only some close relatives and friends. But to everyone I met I mentioned my wonderful experiences in Jamalpur. About half a dozen of my relatives and friends were so impressed by my story that they wanted to learn meditation immediately. One of them was Tej Karan, my wife's maternal uncle. He later went to Jamalpur to meet Baba and his experiences there played no small part in bringing a very special lady to Ananda Marga, of which more in the next chapter.

Apart from Tej Karan there are only a few devoted *margiis* (followers of Ananda Marga) in Kota and yet Baba paid at least three very memorable visits to this city. To me this is a sign that the place itself has some special spiritual quality.

Baba's first visit to Kota in 1966 is memorable in many ways. The degree and depth of love that he showered on those who came in contact with him there was immense. Long after Baba's visit, the retired Assistant Revenue Commissioner Mr Sethi, who was a *Namdhari Sikh*, related to me how he would sometimes have very sweet and blissful dreams of Baba. He was about eighty when Baba paid his first visit to Kota and not a very regular *sadhak* (spiritual practitioner) before or after the visit. Nevertheless, somewhere in his subconscious Baba's image got stuck permanently. There are many such examples where simple and honest people, though they never became followers of Ananda Marga, were struck by Baba's presence.

On Baba's first visit to Kota my wife and I travelled with him on the train from Delhi. We had reserved a first class car with four berths, of which the lower two were for Baba and his personal assistant and the upper two for me and my wife. This was the most memorable train journey of our lives. To have our guru exclusively to ourselves for eight long hours! What more can be wished for?

To begin with, we were sitting on the floor of the compartment and chatting freely with Baba on random topics including higher-level politics. Baba told us that a *sadhak* should engage in a ceaseless fight against evil within and without. To this, my wife responded that we could not fight with the cunning and powerful of the world. Our nature was against it. We had no training and aptitude for this kind of struggle. Baba reassured her that he did not mean physical fight. A stage would come, he said, when the evil forces would be divided into belligerent factions and fight amongst themselves to the finish.

'You need not take up arms. All that you have to do is not to join them in their evil design and keep up an attitude of uncompromising opposition and non-cooperation with them'.

Later on, the time came to let Baba rest and go up to our berths. I told my wife that we should sleep on the floor itself, as it was not proper for her as a daughter-in-law to take a higher berth. On hearing my statement, Baba objected. He told Sarla not to hesitate and go up, and that she should rise above men. He was speaking symbolically as well as directly to Sarla, and his words gave her a feeling of immense liberation. Even now she remembers them, and whenever I try to teach my granddaughters or daughters-in-law traditional manners, she reminds me that Baba encourages women to occupy higher posts than men.

On this train journey we made a stopover at the Sawai Madhopur station. Here some employees of the local cement factory gave Baba a tumultuous reception. They had come to the station even though it was past midnight. Leading that group was Mr M. P.

Jain who had recently been initiated. He was very devout and boarded the train to go up to Kota with us. Later on he came to be posted as General Manager of the cement wing of the famous Bajaj Group at Delhi and has remained a strong pillar of Ananda Marga all these years. Baba used to call him *smit-mukh*, meaning 'of a smiling countenance'. Jain and I would often pay joint visits to Baba in Calcutta and whenever Baba would see one of us he would generally enquire about the other, which always gave us immense joy.

The arrangements for Baba's stay had been made in a local *dharamshala*. Visitors were given accommodation in the same building, while the gathering was held in the hall of the nearby multi-purpose higher secondary school. Major Daulat Singh, an elderly devotee from Jaipur, had come to provide transport for Baba, and the Goenkas, a well-known business family from Bombay, stayed with me in my house at Nayapura.

That Baba encouraged the use of local language and songs became evident during this visit. On one occasion, my wife was asking someone to take away the street pups that had entered the building. On hearing this, Baba asked her what 'pups' were called in Hadoti, my wife's mother tongue and the local language of Kota. Sarla had become so much accustomed to speaking Hindi that she could not recollect the local name. After probing for some time Baba said, 'Please call them *ganakras*', which is indeed the Hadoti word for pups.

On another occasion, while serving food to Baba, Sarla requested someone to bring some salt. Baba intervened and asked her to tell him the word for 'salt' in Hadoti. Again Sarla failed to recollect the proper word and Baba reminded her that salt was called *loond* in her mother tongue.

The medium of education and governance in Rajasthan is Hindi. At higher levels in the administration however, in the state secretariat for example, English is used to make notes and communicate decisions. This has resulted in a hidden sense of pride and superiority amongst those who speak English. And at another level, Hindi speaking people are regarded superior to those who speak only their local language. This false linguistic hierarchy in society has lead to the neglect of folk songs and literature and is still today adversely affecting the creativity and expression of a large number of people. Baba did not like this sense of false pride arising from the use of an alien language. He was for the flowering of local literature and the preservation of every linguistic heritage.

As a result, the ladies had adopted local devotional songs to welcome Baba in Hadoti, which they sang before every gathering. In this process, incidentally, we also got a glimpse into the vastness of Baba's linguistic knowledge. Later, on another occasion, Baba gave a formal statement that he knew around two hundred languages of the world.

As it happened, one of the days during Baba's visit fell on Holi, the famous North-Indian colour festival of spring. Baba was in a pleasant mood that day. We put a plateful of *gulal,* a red coloured powder, at his feet and, once he had touched it, we applied the powder to each other's foreheads, sang songs and danced. In his speech, Baba talked about the global as well as the mythological significance of Holi. He said that in all the cold countries of the world the end of the bitter winter is celebrated with great gaiety and festivities. Life takes a creative turn, the birds chirp and sing, new shoots emerge from the earth and on the branches of trees, and farmers sow seeds for the year's crop. In some countries, they burn a bonfire in each village, a roughly made wooden structure is covered with sheepskin and burnt with abandon and great celebration.

In the colder northern parts of India, winter is also given a ceremonial farewell. In ancient times, according to the myth of Holi, there lived a demon king named Hiranyakashipu. He had been granted a boon that made it almost impossible for him to be killed and consequently he had become arrogant and power hungry. He demanded that people stop worshipping the gods and start praying to him. His own son, Prahlada, however, was an ardent devotee of Vishnu and continued to worship the god despite Hiranyakashipu's threats. When all the demon king's attempts to kill Prahlada failed, Hiranyakashipu finally ordered his young son to sit on a pyre on the lap of his demon sister Holika. Holika was a cannibal and loved to eat children from the locality. She too had been granted a boon: hers would protect her from fire. But, to the people's utter amazement and joy it was Holika who was burnt to ashes by the fire, while Prahlad remained unscathed. His devotion and complete surrender to Vishnu had protected him from the flames. Thereafter, this triumph of good over evil was celebrated in a spirit of emancipation and gaiety.

Baba then traced the history of Holi through the ages. In the beginning, people would play with the flowers that were abundant on the trees at the start of spring. Gradually, they began to make coloured water from the flowers and the tradition of throwing the coloured water on one another developed. Through the passage of time this custom degenerated into throwing mud and dust on one another. In addition, people colour the faces of friends with black and blue powders, singing and dancing wildly and feasting abundantly.

We too enjoyed a lavish feast that day. Mrs Rathi from Calcutta was an expert in preparing Bengali dishes, and on this occasion cooked up a storm. After Baba had eaten a small portion, we took the rest as *prasad* with great pleasure.

The next day, as we started for a walk with Baba, none of us could have imagined that he would take us to an as yet undiscovered archaeological site. Baba directed us to a dam on the bank of a small river. As we stood on the top of a big cliff overlooking the river bank, a *sadhu* emerged from below. He was in his forties or so and had matted hair like any other mendicant. He told us that he lived in the caves on the bank of the river. When the *sadhu* was about to leave, Baba requested Dada Raghunathji to go with him to see the caves and report back. So Raghunathji followed the *sadhu* down the rocky path, while we continued our walk on the top of the cliff.

After about twenty minutes, Raghunathji returned and began to describe the caves, which were many and quite impressive. On the walls of the caves were paintings which looked very old. He had brought a small sample from one of the caves. Baba examined the small piece, on which were painted little figures resembling men and animals. He told us that these were ancient paintings and an archaeological treasure, as they must be dating back to the pre-Shiva period, some seven to eight thousand years ago.

This proved to be a unique and important find. Later on, the relevant department of the government of India recognised its importance and declared the caves an archaelogical site and protected monument.

The following day we went to Rawatbhata, an important dam site on the bank of the Chambal some forty or fifty km away from Kota. There are several nuclear reactor and heavy-water plants at Rawatbhata. The road is a zigzag, a winding beautiful track with hills on either side.

Just before the Rawatbhata dam site, there are many relics of ancient temples. When we stopped at these temples, Baba took my notebook and made several different drawings of the ancient art of constructing temples. He explained the main features of the temple architecture through the ages, describing the puranic, Jain, Buddhist and tantrik temples and lucidly elaborating on their main distinguishing features.

He explained that the temples' Buddhist and Jain idols were mildly modified after the advent of Shankaracharya, so that they would resemble Hindu gods and goddesses. A small Shivalinga had been installed on the head of a Buddha statue and the temple converted into a Shiva temple.

On return from the temples, Dada Ramanandaji drove Baba's Mercedes fast along the winding hilly road, but I with my Fiat was unable to keep up with them. Having had insufficient sleep for the last couple of days, I felt incredibly tired and drove slowly. Only the cool wind from the hills kept me awake. Tej Karanji, Dandotiyaji and Jagdish were with me in the car. And as we approached the skirt of a wayside hamlet, there lay a big pile of boulders and stones on the road. I could not see this clearly with my sleepy eyes. The car went headlong towards the boulders, but miraculously it took a high jump and we were across the heap in a second. All four of us were completely shaken.

When I reached Kota and met Ramanandaji, Baba's PA, he told me how Baba was anxiously enquiring about us. Then he conveyed to me Baba's instructions that I should not drive a vehicle between noon and three o'clock, for that was the time when drowsiness usually came to me.

The most memorable event of Baba's first visit to Kota, was the gathering of *margiis* on the roof of the *dharamshala* building on the morning of Baba's departure to Delhi. It was around 10am. A cool breeze was blowing. Men, women and children had all gathered to see Baba off. As he climbed up on to the roof and sat on the small wooden cot spread out for him, a gush of spiritual vibration filled the air and thrilled everyone sitting there. Someone began to sing the departing song sung by the *gopis* when Krishna left Gokul for Mathura. It was a very poignant song, full of the pangs of separation. The language was Bhojpuri and it was rendered with great devotion. Slowly and slowly many in the gathering began to sob and cry, until tears rolled down almost every face in the gathering. I saw that Baba's face shone with emotion. His whole frame was vibrating to the sobs and cries of the audience.

This expression of deep *bhav* continued for about ten to fifteen minutes and it seemed as though we lost our feeling of self for that short while as we were soaked in sweet sadness. Old and young, ladies and gents, *sadhaks* and non-*sadhaks*, everyone was infected by the atmosphere. Baba also was visibly moved and two dadas had to help him get up. He began to walk slowly towards the car and like a magnet he drew everyone with him. There was a rush towards him and none was enough in their senses to control the crowd. One Nepali boy, who did not get space to climb down the stairs, jumped to the ground from the first floor and surprisingly was not hurt.

With some difficulty Baba reached the waiting car below, and everyone gathered around it, not wanting him to go.

Sarla and I went to the station to see Baba off. We sat with him in the waiting room, wishing for some way to delay his departure. Sarla requested him to give us a few more hours, as we were unable to see him go so soon. And lo and behold, it was announced that the frontier mail would be two hours late and we were able to put off our parting a little longer.

***

On Baba's second visit to Kota he came by Dakota aircraft. I was planning to travel with him and had purchased my tickets for the flight, but unfortunately I suddenly developed very high malarial fever and had to drop my plan. My wife and my younger brother's wife, Lalli, seized this opportunity to travel with him. On the plane Sarla sat next to Baba, blissfully listening to his descriptions of the history and geography of the places that passed below. My brother's wife, however, became increasingly impatient that Sarla did not speak to Baba about the depressed state of our son's mind, nor did she request Baba to cure him. Finally, on her frequent and persistent prodding, Sarla hesitatingly mentioned the name of our youngest son to him. Almost immediately, Baba rose from his seat, went to the toilet and on return sat next to his PA.

Thereupon, Sarla told Lalli that Baba did not like such requests. These requests implied that he was unaware of our difficulties, which was incorrect. He knew everything and would remove our troubles at the appropriate time if he so wished. But Baba never liked prayer as a means to removing worldly problems. He wanted us to reap the fruits of our actions. As a guru he would help remove the cause of our troubles forever by spiritually uplifting us and giving us the strength to bear the failures and misfortunes of life with a balanced mind.

***

Baba's third and last visit to Kota in 1984 was quite eventful for me. This visit was in connection with a chain of seventeen visits he paid to various places, covering cities in Bihar, Uttar Pradesh, Delhi, Himachal Pradesh, Madhya Pradesh and Rajasthan. One of the cities he visited during this tour was Jaipur, where I was living at the time. The decision where to hold the next *Dharma Maha Chakra* after Jaipur was taken in the night after the *darshan* was over. Baba's personal staff and the dadas were in favour of going to Gwalior from Jaipur, but Baba put his weight for Kota and thus Kota was selected as the venue of the next gathering. As soon as this decision was taken, Tej Karanji and Jagdish, who were both from Kota, rushed back to Kota by night train. All the arrangements had to be made within just twenty-four hours, but Tej Karanji was confident that all would be well. And so it was.

It is said that the Lord moves with *ridhi* (growth) and *sidhi* (success) at his command and that his devotees need not exert when arranging for his welcome. Though Kota had hardly three or four *margiis* with small financial means, all arrangements for the big gathering were made in just twenty-four hours and were far superior to those available in Jaipur, though in Jaipur there were some fifty *margii* families.

I started for Kota some two to three hours earlier than Baba's scheduled departure, with my wife and Mrs Rathi of Calcutta as co-passengers. I was driving my Fiat fast in the hope of contributing to the arrangements for Baba's stay and to welcome him when he arrived in Kota.

But as I reached the clock tower circle in the heart of Tonk, a town some two hours' drive from Jaipur, I had a bad accident. A truck coming from the opposite direction collided directly with my car. For a moment I was stunned. I looked back, the passengers were shaken but safe. I got out and looked at the bonnet and engine. The front was smashed. Other parts were also partially damaged. In a neighbouring shop I picked up the phone and rang the District Collector, informing him of my plight. He immediately sent someone to take the car to a nearby repair workshop. The mechanic at the workshop said that it would take at least an hour or so, as some parts would need replacing. I urged him to work as fast as possible.

We sat in the workshop while the vehicle was being repaired and after about half an hour, I saw Baba's Mercedes speeding towards Kota. My dream of welcoming him was dashed; still I wanted to rush there as soon as possible.

I started again from Tonk and raised the speed with a view to be with Baba as soon as possible. The road was smooth and we were speeding for Kota when after about one and a half hour's drive near Deoli one of my tyres burst with a loud blast. We looked for a tyre repair shop and it took another thirty to forty minutes before we could continue our journey.

It seemed we were facing unusual hindrances in reaching Kota. I called up Tej Karan to inform him about the delay and found out that Baba had twice enquired whether I had arrived. This gave me renewed strength in continuing my movement towards Baba.

It was nearly two in the afternoon when we finally reached Tej Karan's house. After a quick wash and some refreshments, we went to Baba's residence nearby. By then Baba had finished his lunch and started 'personal contacts'.

In the evening Baba was to be taken to the Chambal for his evening walk. I offered my car, as the other car was carrying security volunteers. But unfortunately, on this route again we had not one but another two flat tyres. I was sorry that Baba was put to such inconvenience. But thankfully we all managed to fit into the second car and reach our destination, while my car was yet again sent to the workshop for the necessary repairs.

At the Chambal, Baba enjoyed the sight of the deep azure water. We walked along the barrage, while he told us the history of the river. Like the Ganges, the Chambal was a very ancient river. In the distant past many animal sacrifices were held on its banks. Whenever a big *yagya* was performed somewhere upstream in the dense jungles, the river was covered for miles by the bloody hides of wild boar. Because of these hides and skins the river's name became Charmanavati, *charm* meaning hide in Sanskrit. Baba spoke out against these kind of animal sacrifices and explained that in ancient India they were very much prevalent.

The following day after breakfast, we took Baba to Adhar Shila and Bhitariya Kund. Adhar Shila is a huge rock hanging precariously over a cliff on the bank of the Chambal. It looks as though it is about to fall into the river. According to local folklore, the rock was thrown there by a demon to block the flow of the river and destroy the people of the area. A Muslim saint living in a nearby cave on the riverbank saw the menacing rock about to topple into the river, and with his spiritual powers he stopped it in its tracks. So it hangs till today. After his death the saint was buried next to the rock.

When we reached Adhar Shila, Baba stood for some time looking at the hanging rock and the grave of the saint. He told us that the saint had been an advanced occult practitioner and could stop the falling rock midway with his occult powers. Then he called the *maulvi*, the Muslim priest, who was the keeper of the grave, and enquired which kind of *namaz* he was practising. The man did not know that there was any other kind of *namaz* than the one he performed. We too were surprised. So Baba described both types of *namaz* and explained in which regions of the world they were practised. As we left, the *maulvi* bowed to Baba in reverence.

We continued our walk down to Bhitariya Kund, which was some fifty feet below, on the bank of the Chambal. While climbing down Baba explained the levels of rock formations and told us that in rocks like these the possibility of digging artesian wells was very strong.

At the bottom we reached a Shiva temple, where a Hindu priest was reciting some Sanskrit verses as part of his *puja*. Here there was an idol of Ganesh, which was widely worshipped by people. Baba stopped at the site for a while and when the *pujari* had finished his prayers, Baba requested him to recite the proper Ganesh verse for us. But the poor man did not know the correct verse. He was reciting whichever holy verses he had learnt. He also was unaware of what the two small idols on either side of the Ganesh statue represented. So Baba recited the Ganesh verse clearly and loudly as it is written in the *Puranas* and explained that the two female idols represented the two wives of Ganesh. Impressed by Baba's knowledge the *pujari* touched Baba's feet.

I don't recall when exactly, but once, while walking on the bank of the Chambal, Baba remarked, 'I love the soil of Kota very much'. He foretold that one day people from many different countries would sing *kiirtan* there and dance in great devotion and bliss.

Baba at the Jaipur airport. Sarla is sitting beside him on his right.

Spirituality is not a utopian ideal but a practical philosophy which can be practised and realized in day-to-day life, however mundane it be. Spirituality stands for evolution and elevation, and not for superstition, inaction or pessimism. All fissiparous tendencies and group or clan philosophies which tend to create the shackles of narrow-mindedness are in no way connected with spirituality and should be discouraged. That which leads to broadness of vision alone should be accepted. Spiritual philosophy does not recognize any distinctions and differentiations unnaturally made between one human being and another, and stands for universal fraternity.

5 June 1959, Jamalpur

Aunty

The city of Udaipur is enchanting in its scenic beauty and glorious in its history. It is quite rightly a famous tourist spot in Rajasthan. Due to its many deep and beautiful lakes, it is also called the Lake City. Among the lakes close to the city are Pichola, Swarup Sagar and Fateh Sagar. The Pichola is known for a most exquisite hotel, the Lake Palace, which is situated on an island in the lake. Many famous kings and warriors of Mewar are associated with Udaipur, among them the great warrior and freedom fighter, Rana Pratap. He was one of only a few who refused to surrender to the great might of the Mughal empire. Akbar had extended the boundaries of his Mughal empire up to the far south and east of the country and subjugated almost all the Rajput clans, except the Sisodias of Mewar.

It was to Udaipur that I was transferred in 1964 as additional commissioner of commercial taxes, Rajasthan. I lived in a lovely bungalow near the Fateh Sagar lake. It stood on a small hill and was wind-swept throughout the year. I found this house especially congenial for meditation. I look back at my days in Udaipur with great fondness, as it was a spiritually fruitful time. All three of my sons took initiation and experienced the joys of meditation during our time there. In those days my face glowed with happiness and this impressed friends and strangers alike. One such friend was Dr Fateh Singh, the retired Principal of Herbert College in Kota. He was a staunch Arya Samaji and a renowned vedic scholar. He had been my Principal when I was working as a lecturer in that college. When I related to him my experiences with Baba, he was keen to be initiated, and observed, 'Your face is the biggest proof of the efficacy of this *sadhana* that you are doing'.

Another person who was initiated during my time in Udaipur was Mrs Vimala Vashishta. She lived on the top of the hill with her son-in-law Mr P. C. Mishra, the police superintendent of the district. Mrs Vashistha was already an experienced traveller on the spiritual path. She was a dedicated follower of Guru Ramdasji, who had quite an influence on many families in Bombay and was famous far and wide. Having renounced her husband and family in Bombay, she had gone to her guru's ashram and there lived the life of a mendicant. Her family was from the upper middle class, her husband had a lucrative government job, and all her sons and daughters, save the youngest son, were grown up and settled in life.

But when Ramdasji left his body Mrs Vashistha felt sad and forlorn. The charge of the ashram went to another lady disciple and so she came to stay with her daughter and son-in-law in Udaipur.

In those days, I was in such an ecstatic spiritual state that life felt like a bed of roses. Every Sunday evening we held a gathering with devotional songs and intense meditation at our house, and although the attendance was limited to fifteen people, the sounds of *hunkar,* laughter and weeping from the attendees were so loud that strangers walking on the road below were bewildered.

Mrs Vashistha heard about our weekly *satsang* and we heard about her spiritual interests. We requested her to join our gathering and participate in the devotional singing and meditation. After some hesitation, she agreed. Her first experience of the *satsang* was vibrating, but confusing. She had spent all her life in a religious environment, but had never witnessed a group of *grihasthas* (people leading a family life) so advanced or involved in deep devotion. Many doubts came to her mind, but the fact that I was a civil officer of high status helped her overcome her confusion. After all, like her son-in-law, I was performing my duties as a government officer and my sons were all good students. The others at *satsang* too were civil servants or advocates and were respected in society. Her curiosity was awakened and we tried to persuade her to take initiation and merge wholeheartedly in the spirit of our weekly gathering. The fact that she already had a guru and had been teaching his school of meditation for quite some time prevented her from changing horses midstream. But her mind was increasingly attracted to try this new school of meditation, which had such a profound impact on young and old.

The struggle within her mind, whether to join and accept a new guru or continue as before, intensified and finally resulted in a profound dream. In the dream her guru appeared before her and asked her to touch the feet of a young mendicant who was standing nearby. As she did this, her guru told her that she had touched infinity. Then he disappeared. Mrs Vashistha did not quite follow the significance of the dream until she came to my house the next noon and found that very same mendicant from her dream sitting before her. She then realised that it was her guru's instruction to take initiation from this young man.

An entirely new vista opened up after her initiation. She not only liked the new meditation but also the philosophy propounded by Anandamurtiji. She used to talk to my middle son Mukt about philosophy and his experiences during meditation. He was perhaps only 15 years old then, but was well versed with the Ananda Marga philosophy and many of the principal religious texts, such as the Gita, the Bible and the Koran.

In the afternoons she began to call my wife to the lakeside house of her friend, Mrs Singhal. There they had long discussions on God, Avatar, Krishna, Shiva, the Ramayana and the Mahabharata. My wife was not learned in any sense of the term. She was literate but no more, and had mostly heard about the stories of our great epics, the Ramayana and the Mahabharata. But she had tasted the nectar of spirituality and had grasped the essence of the divine. Her simple but wise reactions to the questions put to her by Mrs Vashistha and Mrs Singhal impressed them and they both began to veer towards the worship of the formless, rather than the idols and pictures of Lord Rama, Krishna and Shiva.

These were the days when my wife's maternal uncle, Tej Karan Sharma, had gone to Jamalpur and, on my request, was recording his daily experiences on a post card and sending the same to me. He was a non-religious type, very blunt and direct, and did not believe in the ostentations of traditional worship. In the evenings after meals, I would go for a walk on the bank of one of the lakes and read out Tej Karan's letter to those with me. Our group often included Mrs Vashistha, who keenly listened to these letters.

Then one fine morning, instead of a postcard I received a long letter from Tej Karan. It contained his transcendental experience of one Sunday in the small sitting room of the Jamalpur ashram. He recounted in a simple and direct language how a ray of light from Baba's eyes entered his forehead as he was listening to his discourse. This divine light spread throughout Tej Karan's frame and, vibrating almost violently, it moved up and down his spinal cord at a terrific speed. He felt a blissful sensation rising in his mind. Falling to the floor, he began to shake violently as one does when one gets an electric shock. He was engulfed in blinding light and began to shed tears uncontrollably. All who were present in the room witnessed his condition.

After some time Baba gave instructions to Dada Abhedanandaji and then he left the room as usual. A couple of curious bystanders touched Tej Karan and in doing so they too began to tremble, as if the current was passing into them through the touch. Tej Karan must have remained in that blissful state for a couple of hours. When he regained his senses, Dada explained that Baba had raised his *kundalini* by simply looking at him.

As I read his letter, I felt as though some small part of that energy was passing through me as well. Mrs Vashistha too was profoundly moved by Tej Karan's experience.

To these experiences was added my wife's supernatural behaviour during one gathering at our residence. That particular evening while doing meditation, she began to behave abnormally. She started laughing and crying uncontrollably and talked of the 'enchanting sound of a flute'. No one else could hear the sound of a flute, and when Mrs Vashistha tried to touch my wife, the latter strongly repelled the advance. Raising both of her hands as if she was wading through a crowd, Sarla uttered, 'Get away! Give me space, let me see the Lord'.

She remained in this ecstatic state for nearly half an hour and we wondered what it could signify. She later recounted, that she was transported to a hilly and beautiful green surrounding where she heard the enchanting melody of a flute. In a thatched hall a congregation had collected to hear Baba speak and she wanted to enter the hall to get a better view of him seated on the dais inside.

A few days later an Ananda Marga *sanyasi* came to visit us, and he told us that Baba had gone to Assam to give a talk there. The details he gave of the place and gathering matched the description my wife had given of her ecstatic vision during meditation.

Now Mrs Vashistha was convinced that this was not an ordinary meditation or an ordinary guru. The desire to go to Jamalpur to get a close glimpse of this divine personality became very strong in her. However, her health was not good in those days and she struggled even to come from her son-in-law's bungalow to our house. She had pain in her joints and was suffering from other ailments too. Nevertheless, she decided to take the plunge and go to Jamalpur to see Baba.

What happened to her there is now history. She decided to devote her life to Baba's mission and became the first *sanyasini* or nun in Ananda Marga. She later went on to become the chief of the Women's Welfare Department of Ananda Marga and is more famously known as Aunty Ananda Bharatiji. For about twenty-five years she headed the ladies wing of Ananda Marga and gave it a very stable and enlightened foundation. Workers from all over the world used to come to this motherly devotee for inspiration and solace.

Aunty Ananda Bharatiji

In the psychic world Parama Purusa has infinite power. All longings and thoughts are reflected on His mental mirror. Any action one performs, any thought one is trying to materialize, is immediately reflected on the vast mental mirror. One cannot keep anything secret from Him. If a small piece of stone is thrown into the vast ocean it creates tiny ripples on its smooth surface. This event, although trivial, does not remain unknown to the ocean. Even the least vibration created within the unit mind is immediately known to the Macrocosmic Mind, for the unit mind is within the vast Macrocosmic Mind.

26 November 1966, Midnapur

The Stranger

On one summer day, I felt a sudden and strong impulse to visit Baba in Jamalpur. For some reason that I fail to recall now, I felt very sad and depressed on that day. I packed a small bag and left for the station. There was no chance to get a reserved seat at this late stage. When the train arrived I attempted to board one of the compartments for passengers without reservations, but it was packed beyond capacity. In my downcast state of mind, I couldn't bear the thought of suffering the long journey in such a hell hole. So I boarded a compartment intended for passengers with reservations instead.

There I saw a well built young man sleeping on one of the lower berths. I put my bag under the berth and squeezed myself on to the edge of the berth next to the young man's feet.

Some minutes after the train had departed the young man woke up. 'Who are you?' he demanded in a stern voice. Very nervously I replied, 'I had to go urgently, but couldn't get a reservation. If you can give me just a foot of space, I won't disturb you at all'.

The young man now proceeded to scold me. 'You look like an elderly and honest fellow. Couldn't you bother to ask the ticket collector whether there is an empty berth? Is this a way to travel? What about those like me who took the pains to pay for a reservation?'

Full of guilt I listened silently. What could have I said? The young man was right. Then suddenly he got up and offered me a glass of water. I thanked him but declined his offer and quietly sat with my head hung in shame and my eyes cast to the floor. I was mentally preparing myself for the next outburst and decided that I should perhaps sit on the floor instead.

As I sat mulling these thoughts, the young man took out a bed sheet from his bag and said, 'Etiquette demands that I sleep on the floor and give you my berth'. I was stunned by this change of heart. 'No, no, please stay. I will see if I can find a place somewhere else', I protested.

But he would have none of it. He emptied his berth and made me take it. His voice was commanding, allowing no argument on the matter. Utterly embarrassed I lay down on the berth, as he spread his sheet on the floor underneath. Extremely tired and worried I soon fell fast asleep.

When I woke up a few hours later, the young man had disappeared. I asked the person on the berth opposite mine, if he had seen the young man leave, but he seemed entirely unaware of the whole incident. Instead he suggested cynically that in these bad times a ruffian would go to any length to steal people's luggage. My luggage, however, was untouched. I thought to myself that ruffians don't hide sweet love behind a stern voice.

Upon meeting Baba in Jamalpur, his first words to me were: 'Mangal Bihari, you didn't suffer any inconvenience during your journey, did you?'

The greatest gain in becoming a moralist is that a man has tremendous moral force. That one has not committed a wrong, is not doing so nor will do so — this very awareness generates in one a force, the moral force.

19 November 1967, Ranchi

Moral Force

Tej Karan and I were returning from Ananda Nagar, after attending a *Dharma Maha Cakra* there. We had reserved two lower berths and were enjoying our discussion of the various incidents at the gathering. The train was quickly filling with passengers who were without reservations, and soon we had hardly any space to sit on our own reserved berths. We were passing cynical comments on the frustrating situation. Though it was prohibited, a number of people were smoking one cigarette after another. The air was heavy with smoke and it was increasingly difficult to breathe in the overcrowded compartment. Our condition was miserable, but how could we pick a fight with so many?

In the meantime our attention was caught by a soldier in uniform, who sat at the window opposite us, smoking like a chimney. He was quite muscular and looked fearsome. It seemed that the slightest irritation might blow his fuse. But Baba's words about standing up to anti-social behaviour were ringing in our ears.

Tej Karan by nature is impatient and impulsive, and in those days he was still a young man. He got up and started explaining the ill effects of smoking to the soldier. The soldier nonchalantly ignored him. Finally, Tej Karan placed his hand on the soldier's shoulder and asked him to stop smoking, as it was affecting us adversely. In response the soldier puffed out a mouth-full of smoke right in Tej Karan's face. The situation was getting out of hand.

But before I could intervene, Tej Karan snatched the cigarette from the soldier's mouth and threw it out of the window. Anything could happen now.

I got up and pulled Tej Karan back to his berth. The soldier was silent and glared at us for a very long minute. Then he put his hand inside his pocket. My heart was racing now.

I was afraid that he would pull out a knife or a revolver. But instead he pulled out a pack of cigarettes and to our great astonishment he threw it out of the window. Then he got up and told two other smoking passengers that it was a crime to smoke on the train without the permission of the co-passengers. The two passengers were visibly scared by the soldier's stern challenge and quickly stubbed out their cigarettes.

Tej Karan and I couldn't believe our eyes. I then remembered that Baba had once said, 'No matter how strong the evil force be, it will have to bow down to the moral force'.

The main and inevitable aim of every sadhaka is not to enjoy the nectar of devotion by himself or herself, but to distribute it all around. Sadhakas are eager to share with others the bliss which they enjoy.

22 January 1971, Ranchi

Our Guest

I was exceptionally fortunate that Baba accepted my poor hospitality not only once or twice but four times. This life of mine has been blessed beyond imagination. I feel overwhelmed when I remember his presence in the various houses that were my home during my life. Unfortunately all of them were rented residences and now I can enter them only on request and for a very brief duration.

Some experiences were common amongst all of Baba's visits. So for example, we were never one-hundred per cent sure whether Baba would come until he actually arrived at our doorstep. There were always others competing for the opportunity to host him and many were as keen in their efforts as my wife and I.

Once in Delhi, his visit was so sudden and unexpected that we had hardly enough time to arrange for his stay. Normally, we would make advance preparations and when he came to stay we felt that our efforts had been fruitful. Our residence in Delhi on this occasion was sparsely furnished, meagrely decorated and not very spacious. We could only offer Baba a rather small room with an ineffective cooler that spewed vapour and left the air suffocating and sultry.

Whenever Baba stayed with us, the house was flooded with people and if we wanted to rest or sleep, we had to find some small space wherever we could. This applied to all the members of the family and many a time my children would go and stay with friends in neighbouring houses.

The management of Baba's room was always taken over by his personal secretary for the duration of that specific tour. The personal secretary alone could arrange appointments and would restrict entry to Baba's room according to the occasion. In spite of this, there was ample 'smuggling in' by various devotees on one pretext or another, especially when food was being served to Baba. Someone would come with a spoon, another with a glass of water and a third would enter the room with additional supplements to the lunch or dinner. Whether or not the item they brought was used by Baba ceased to matter once they were through the door and sitting at the table with him. They had no interest in eating with Baba, but just wished to be close to him. The security personnel could not make an unpleasant scene around the dining table by turning them out, since they were charged with maintaining a pleasant atmosphere while Baba was taking his meals.

Though he was served several dishes each day, morning and evening, Baba's diet was very moderate. He would take very little from each dish, just enough to appreciate the taste and cooking, to the delight of the ladies.

Generally the problem for cooks is deciding the content of the menu. What vegetables should be selected for the morning and evening? In the case of Baba's kitchen, the ladies often prepared their own favourite dishes for him. At times, however, my wife would go and ask him which vegetables he preferred for lunch or dinner. On one such occasion, when Sarla enquired which dish she should prepare, Baba told her with an amused smile: 'Mangal Bihari has put up a chart of vegetables that are to be cooked on mornings and evenings of all the seven days in the week. Why don't you follow that chart?' My wife was surprised that Baba had come to know about that small hand written chart, which not long ago I had prepared and put up as much for her convenience as to save myself the bother of frequent discussions on the subject.

Baba's routine was very taxing, but not a line of vexation or tiredness was ever visible on his smiling face. Right from three o'clock in the morning up to eleven or twelve in the night he was busy with one meeting or another.

On one of the nights while staying with us in Delhi, Baba gave *avadhuta* initiations to more than ten people in our house. Before they entered Baba's room to be initiated into the advanced spiritual practice, my wife would put the vermilion mark on the forehead of the candidate and give them one or two garlands made out of *rudraksh* beads. On their return, their saffron dress was ready for them to put on and they became *avadhutas*. We witnessed this with some awe and much bliss. In fact, that room in our house at South Extension in Delhi became an ideal place for meditation practice, imbued as it was with conducive spiritual vibrations.

In between his busy daily work schedule, Baba would come and talk sweetly with those waiting in the hall or on the verandah. On these occasions, he would bless many *sadhaks* with a touch or a look, sometimes giving them miraculous spiritual experiences.

Baba never carried more than two changes of clothes in his small attaché, and each morning and evening there was a competition amongst close devotees to wash, dry and press his *dhoti* and *kurta*. His clothes were always simple, not richly embroidered silk, but plain white cotton, easy to wash by hand and to dry and press.

We noted during Baba's stay in our house that he would take at least four baths every day: one early in the morning, another at about midday, a third in the late afternoon and the last before going to bed. These four baths were like tonics for him and he would wash out whatever tiredness he might be feeling. After each bath he would begin his work with redoubled vigour and freshness. Baba's schedule was long and very crowded, and yet he found time to chat for some time with each member of the family in an informal manner. To everyone he gave the impression that he was one of us, an ordinary member of our family.

Every day Baba would go for two long walks in a nearby garden or park, on which up to four people would accompany him. Curious neighbours, attracted by the crowd and the charged atmosphere, gathered at the gate, and while passing Baba would give them a broad smile and a wave of his hand. Baba's chats on his walks were informal yet highly informative and instructive. He would often discuss a local political, economic or social situation, and offer deep analysis and pertinent solutions.

It was known that walking was part of Baba's rest time and that no one was to raise deep philosophical questions or personal problems during this time. However, when a serious matter was weighing on someone's mind, Baba would often bring up the matter himself, and gently probe and offer advice.

When Baba would leave our house to give a discourse in some hall, my wife would be the last to leave the house for the meeting. She would finish up everything in the kitchen, pack Baba's lemon water and lock up the house. As such, she would often take the last vehicle to reach the meeting place. She would also be the first to leave the hall, so that she could prepare Baba's room before he returned. Thus her mind was not fully engaged in hearing Baba's speech. So Baba would find some time to tell her about the subject of his talk or discourse afterwards. In this manner, she remained up to date with his discourses and often corrected us about the substance of his talk.

The string of personal contacts, the long queues of people waiting their turn to see Baba, and the vivid and varied discussions after each person had had Personal Contact with Baba was a wonderful experience — all happening under my roof. Many a time I would see people going into *samadhi* after their Personal Contact, and the pleasant memory of it is still fresh in my mind. I would offer them a glass of cool water or a cup of light tea after they came out of their trance.

In between his other activities, Baba would discuss with those dadas and didis who were assigned social service work abroad, the particulars of the countries they were headed to. He would advise on the dominant characteristics of the people there. Sometimes he would recommend that they meet a particular person who would be helpful to their work. Young men and women who had never in their life boarded an aeroplane, and whose English was poor to say the least, were full of confidence and zeal, eager to do missionary work in lands they knew little to nothing about. And despite a multitude of obstacles they succeeded in their endeavours.

To sum up, during Baba's visits, my family and I were transported from the normal mundane atmosphere of our daily life to a rarer, miraculous and undreamed of spiritual atmosphere, where wonderful things happened as if they were everyday events.

Baba stayed with us like an ordinary guest, demanding nothing, but giving so much precious time, wisdom and spiritual experiences to all who came to see him.

How does one cross the ocean of bhava? It is insurmountable. You do not possess energy and strength in your hands and feet to cross this bhava samudra (sea of reactions). So it will be better if you can get a good boat or a good steamer just to cross this ocean. Oh Parama Purusa, Thou art a ship, and I take shelter in this ship. I will cross the ocean, and I will go to the other bank; it is by your mercy that I will be able to do this. I will take shelter in you.

4 August 1978, Patna

Unseasonal Floods

October is a month of festivities and celebrations in Bengal. The monsoons are over, the surroundings are lush green and the rice crop has ripened in the fields, turning the place into a golden country. The weather is mild and a gentle breeze blows health and happiness into all hearts.

But on this particular October morning, when I got down from the train at Calcutta's Howrah Junction, it was unbearably sultry. I had come to Calcutta for Baba's *darshan* and was headed for the Tiljala ashram, where I was planning to stay for the duration of my visit. I collected my luggage and came out of the station looking for a cab to take me to Tiljala. As usual, you have either to stand in an interminable queue in the sun and wait for a regular cab or fall into the hands of those who promise quick departure at a premium, but actually keep you waiting until the cab is overfilled. Once your luggage is in the hands of these cheats, you are virtually at their mercy. The taxi-union leader will snub and abuse you if you try to be smart and quarrelsome.

Fortunately, someone suggested that I take a steamer part of the way and then continue on from where the cabs were more readily available. So I went across the road and purchased a ticket for the steamer and made myself comfortable on a wooden bench in the boat. Soon, I discovered that the young man sitting close to me was an Ananda Marga *sanyasi* in civil dress. We began to exchange comments about the awful weather at this time of the year. He then revealed to me that the previous night he had dreamt of terrible rains and floods in Calcutta. I explained to him that it was the response of his subconscious to the smothering heat. I did not believe it could rain in late October.

Arriving at the Tiljala ashram, I was taken to the same room in which Acharya Chandranathji, my son's father-in-law and one of the first family-based acharyas in Ananda Marga, was also staying. He kindly arranged for my food and not long after eating, I felt so tired from the journey that I fell asleep. It was a deep sleep and must have lasted a few hours, since when I woke up I observed that the sky was overcast with dark clouds and it was raining cats and dogs.

It rained heavily and continuously all through the night and in the morning we discovered that the compound of the building was covered knee-deep in water. The soak pits that were responsible for the slow absorption of domestic waste water were all filled up and soon began to overflow. The filthy stinking brew was rapidly inundating the ground floor of the ashram. By ten o'clock the kitchen was under about five feet of water and there was no question of getting any cooked food from outside, as both the track leading to the main road and the nearby local market were submerged by the flood-water.

The electric and water supply soon failed, so that we could neither bathe nor drink. Gradually water started entering the rooms of the first floor. The situation looked increasingly grim, as we sat shivering, hungry and thirsty, hoping against all odds that Baba's *darshan* would not be cancelled. The *sanyasi*'s dream, as he had related it to me in the steamer had come true.

In the night it was quite dark, but as Baba's quarter was at a higher level and the generator there was working, Chandranathji and I decided to go there in the hope that Baba might give a *darshan* after all. So we arranged for a small boat and began to row it in the dark, navigating it through the flooded ground floor of the building. Baba's quarter was hardly two or three hundred yards away, but we had to be careful about the pillars and the gates as it was pitch black and the small torch we had threw hardly enough light.

Soon, there was a thud — we had struck a pillar. I became panicky and rushed to the other side of the boat making it topple over and throwing both of us into the muddy, polluted water. We swam back to our room and sat on the wet floor, drenched, shivering and stinking, and feeling much worse off than before our little expedition. There was no dry change of clothes. We were in virtual hell. But Chandranathji's company was a great source of solace and strength. We sat through the night talking, meditating and wondering what was in store for us the next day.

The next morning, Rathiji, a local friend, came in a boat from the city and distributed bread, some snacks and a bottle of drinking water to each person. This was a welcome relief, but it was hardly enough to satisfy our hunger and thirst after two full days trapped in this condition. Many of the inmates left the ashram during the day, but Chandranathji and I held on, thinking that Baba himself was with us.

But now Baba's house too was surrounded with the same filthy water. The following morning, Baba ordered that the ashram be vacated immediately, as the water, the air and the earth had all become poisonous and uninhabitable. A boat was arranged for Baba, duly carpeted and decorated. Baba sat therein on the bench and we, some ten to twelve of us, began to push and row the boat gently out of the gates of his house, through the compound and out through the gates of the ashram, then along the canal which the street had become. This was a chance of a lifetime — we were helping him cross the muddy waters of the world, while he guided us through the ocean of becomings.

As we swam, we saw big snakes, green and brown hanging on the branches of the trees that stood on either side of the road now flooded by the waters. Later on, I wondered that no streak of fear ran through my veins as we steered the boat so close to them. Of course, we were all attentive only toward Baba, who was sitting all through this voyage smiling sweetly with his eyes half closed. Rows of local people stood on their rooftops, and it seemed to me that they were bowing to him. It was a heavenly procession and will remain a precious treasure in my memory all my life. For the time being all my physical pain and feeling of disgust at the filth around me was banished from my mind. I wished that the road from the ashram gate to the highway were to become unending and I could remain near Baba forever. But all too soon we reached the highway and Baba climbed out of the boat and into his car, which was kept ready there by his P.A.

On return from the highway, I could not sit in the boat, much as I wanted to. It was full of *sanyasis* who all wanted to inhale Baba's vibrations and enjoy a royal ride back to the ashram. As I swam back slowly on my own, the feeling of loneliness, uncleanliness, tiresomeness and melancholy again took hold of me. By the time I got back to my room, Acharya Chandranathji had already packed our belongings. Almost immediately, we were taken back in another boat to the road along with others. We took a bus from there and reached Lake Garden in about an hour.

There somehow, we got a little space in a neighbouring house to rest, bathe and change into some borrowed clothes. For the first time in three days, we had something hot to eat. Chandranathji was undisturbed, but within me, a storm was rising from some unknown source. It was a Sunday and in the afternoon

Baba would give his usual *darshan* and weekly discourse.

We walked to Baba's house somewhat before time to secure a seat in the front. But by the time we reached there, the meditation hall was almost full, and we could get only a small sitting space some ten to fifteen rows behind. On this trip, I had not heard Baba at all and I regretted that I was so far away from him and would not be able to enjoy his discourse nor exchange any fortunate glances with him. My heart was full of remorse and sadness that this trip was so 'dry' and tasteless. Soon Baba arrived and sat on his seat. He enquired about everyone's welfare, as was his way. I whispered within myself that I was not at all well physically or mentally.

In the first two or three front rows, some very tall brothers from overseas were almost fully obstructing my view of Baba. Even those who were just in front of me had improved their sitting postures to get a better glimpse of him as he spoke. All hopes of seeing him dwindled. Unless I stood up, there was no chance of watching the expressions on his divine face.

To add to my difficulties, this Sunday Baba was not speaking on his usual linguistic topics, punctuated by humorous anecdotes and almost theatrical postures that made everyone laugh. Today he deviated from his routine and began to explain the abstract philosophy of the Vedas. Baba was mostly speaking in Sanskrit, one of the oldest Indo-Aryan languages. Burdened as I was with my inner sorrow and heavy heart, I soon lost track of the subject altogether. Some ten or fifteen minutes had passed and I was only thinking of all the trouble I had experienced in the train, the boat and the ashram.

And then completely out of context and for no rational reason, Baba suddenly paused in his lecture and asked in a very, very loving voice: 'Do you follow, Mangal Bihari?'

Hearing my name from his lips, suddenly an electric current ran through my whole being. The dam of my sorrow burst, all my pent up gloom began to flow furiously through the gates of my eyes. I was weeping bitterly and heaving sighs loudly. Then in the next moment, I was light and fresh, free of all my gloom and remorse.

Baba continued his discourse unmindful of the miracle his question had worked on me. The discourse was followed by *Prabhat Sangeet* and *guru puja*, after which Baba gave his blessings in the posture of the *varabhaya* mudra. This blessing was given only very rarely at the end of ceremonial meetings or during *Dharma Maha Chakra* gatherings. It worked as a holy balm on my self-inflicted sorrows, and after the flood of my tears, it gave me that thrill and energy which is the very life and soul of spiritual gatherings.

Baba being carried out of Tiljala office in Kolkota after the flood.

He is your Supreme Friend. You are never alone. He can never remain neutral, seeing your sacrifice. Move according to His wishes and you will be relieved of all sufferings.

8 August 1978, Patna

Garden Programme

On another occasion my wife and I went to Calcutta for Baba's *darshan*. We had already booked a reservation for our return journey. This time we were staying with my brother, Satya Bihari.

On Sunday morning, when everyone gathered for general *darshan*, I followed Baba as he was going back to his house. Suddenly he turned back to me and said, 'Today is the garden programme, isn't it? You should also get into it'. Saying this he walked up the stairs to his room on the first floor of the house.

In those days Baba had started a programme to educate people about the enormous collection of trees, shrubs and herbs that had been planted within the compound of his house. The rule was that a set number of people were selected beforehand to attend.

The programme used to start at around noon and last for about two to three hours.

Baba would come down from his room with a small stick. First of all he was introduced to each person who would participate in the programme. After the introduction, he would start with the sandal tree and then move on to the thousands of other plants in the garden, elaborating on their place of origin, medicinal characteristics and other specialities. These plants had been brought here from all over the world, including countries as far away as Brazil, Peru, Thailand and the Philippines. There were some two hundred and fifty types of cacti, a number of varieties of roses, lotus, banana trees and so forth.

I was feeling elated by Baba's unexpected instruction to join the programme. However, I knew that according to the rules, I would not qualify to be part of the group. Firstly, I was not on the list of attendees, and secondly, the opportunity to take part in the programme was not afforded more than once and I had already attended it before. On this day, eight people from Tripura were supposed to join Baba. Their names and addresses had already been communicated to him by Dada Tapeshvarananda.

Nevertheless, after Baba's invitation to join, I ran to Dada Tapeshvarananda and requested him fervently to let me attend the programme. But Dada, who was known to be very strict, did not relent. After trying all sorts of arguments, I even told him that Baba himself had instructed me to join. Still, Dada did not budge, thinking that this was just a ploy of mine.

I had started feeling very bad and under normal circumstances I would have been angry at Dada's stubbornness and left. But I kept remembering Baba's words that I should 'get into' the programme, and that meant that I had to keep persevering. I couldn't give up. I did not go back to Tiljala, nor did I return to my brother's house. Instead, I informed my brother over telephone that I would be attending the garden programme and that he should request my wife to pack and be ready to leave on my return. After all, our train was to depart at 4:30pm and it was nearly midday now.

All but two of the participants from Tripura had assembled for the programme. Dada was trying very hard to find the missing people. But in vain. So he went to Baba with the list of people who had assembled so far and informed him of the two people who were still missing. But instead of coming down Baba was upset with Dada and intended to cancel the programme due to the incomplete group. All this took about an hour. By now it was 1pm.

Another brother from overseas arrived at Lake Gardens, but there was still no sign of the two people from Tripura. It was now nearing Baba's lunch time. Dada again requested Baba to carry on with the programme despite the two absentees. But Dada's helplessness and Baba's anger appeared to increase in the same proportion. When Dada came out of Baba's room I suggested under my breath that he should include the brother from overseas and myself to complete the number of participants. But Dada was still reluctant to break established rules.

Finally, we came to know that Baba had started eating lunch and it now looked very unlikely that the garden programme would take place. The six people from Tripura were dismayed that they would be robbed of the rare fortune to be with Baba. They pleaded with Dada that he do something to make the programme happen or at least give them a chance to see Baba, as they had come from very far simply to avail this opportunity.

Once again I mustered the courage to implore Dada that he believe me; that Baba had indeed requested me to join the programme. Only for this reason had I been hanging around for so long. I urged him to at least go to Baba once more and tell him that there was now a complete group, and to give him the details of the newly added people.

It was nearly 3:30pm when Dada finally made up his mind to follow my suggestion. Baba, it so appeared, was just waiting for this message. He asked Dada to assemble the group and get ready for the programme. Everybody was overjoyed to hear the news. But my happiness had turned into anxiety. Now that Baba was starting the programme at 4pm, how would I catch my train at 4:30pm? The reservation that I had made would go to waste and all other programmes would be disturbed. The opportunity I had been pleading for was now fraught with repercussions. But there was no way out now. Baba was about to come. How could I disappoint so many? And what would Baba think? Due to his wish I was able to join the programme. I was in a weird state of mind.

The consequences of missing my train were appearing in my mind one by one. There was a very important meeting scheduled at office next day, where foreign delegates were to take part. What was I to do now? I was shuddering at the thought, when Baba came down from his room smiling, his small stick in hand. According to the usual protocol everyone was introduced and each of us paid our salutations to him. When Baba looked at me it seemed his smile broadened.

The programme started a few minutes after 4pm and I could hear the horn of my brother's car outside the gates. But neither could he enter the premises nor could I go out. The garden programme for me had become a long and difficult trial. Apparently, this time Baba was taking more time to elaborate than on the previous occasion when I had attended. In all my worry I was neither able to hear Baba nor see the plants. Everyone else was taking notes, but I had neither a diary nor a pen with me. It was as if while wandering in the beautiful valleys of Kashmir I was experiencing the hot desert storms of Rajasthan.

The programme carried on for about three hours. It culminated with the magnificent spectacle of *brahma-kamal,* the grand lotus, which filled everyone with wonder — everyone except me. Even in these cool and calm surroundings I was perspiring. In the end, we all gave our salutations to Baba and left.

On reaching home I made reservations for the next day and went to bed early. I was still feeling distressed that not only did I miss my train but I was also unable to enjoy Baba's programme.

Early the next morning, I read in the paper that some robbers had entered the sleeping compartments of the very same train that I was scheduled to take. In the midnight hours they had looted the passengers and assaulted those who resisted them. One passenger, a soldier, had lost his life during the incident. The emergency handle was pulled and the train stopped. Many passengers were traumatised by the event and wished to be brought back to Calcutta. A shuttle service was being arranged to collect them.

Fortunately, my wife and I were able to take this shuttle service and continue home with the train that we were to take originally.

Now I understood the mystery behind Baba's instruction to join his garden programme. Certainly, it was an interesting way to burn *samskaras*. All anxiety and turmoil was experienced under the loving gaze of his eyes, saving me from the unexpected and dangerous incident.

Your progress in the realm of spirituality, in the realm of intuitionality, depends on His divine grace ... The Vedas say that it depends on divine grace, Guru krpa... And I say, that divine bliss, that divine krpa, that divine compassion, is always being showered upon you, on each and every living being, on each and every animate and inanimate object — but you do not feel it... you are not being drenched by that divine shower, because you are holding the umbrella of vanity upon your head. If you want to be drenched by that divine shower of krpa, you have to remove the umbrella of vanity from your head; just remove it and be drenched. And what is sadhana? Sadhana is just the action of removing this umbrella from upon your head.

November 1966, Ernakulam

He is Me

To my everlasting regret I had missed *dharma samiksha*. This was a personal audience with Baba, in which he would look into the innermost recesses of a person's mind and point out their faults, and in his mysterious way he would help each person overcome the obstacles on their journey toward perfection.

So it was a golden opportunity missed. The monsoons were heavy that year, the road and rail traffic were both disrupted. I succumbed to the threat of discomfort that the two-day journey from Jaipur to Calcutta posed, while others had ignored the fury of the elements and reached there despite the disruptions. Once at the ashram, they had to wait again in interminable queues and weather the sun and rain before their turn came. But when they presented themselves for the miraculous spiritual scrutiny, all their patience and perseverance was duly rewarded. Their body and mind was pierced by the loving laser gaze of the guru who pointed out their major flaws and prescribed new yoga postures, yogic treatments and corrections to their meditation practices. Some devotees came back light like flowers, their entire physical and psychic existence having been overhauled, as it were. The bloom on their faces and the glow in their eyes gave me some idea of what I had missed. But Baba's physical health had suffered a lot during this strenuous process and finally it was declared over. No one knew whether it would be resumed.

I was a little sad and angry at myself for missing such an opportunity. After some months however, I was very much relieved to hear that Baba had started another process called 'special *sadhana*' or '*microvita sadhana*'. He had handpicked some *sadhaks* and started initiating them in this process. I thought that I should not miss this too and rushed to Calcutta to see if I could get myself included in the list. There, I stayed with my brother Satya Bihari, as usual. His house in New Alipur was comparatively close to Baba's residence in Lake Garden and I could come and go back without much physical strain. I waited for days, met Baba's PA and others who attended to Baba's daily chores, but got no clue whether my name was likely to be included. I sat for hours on end in the meditation hall below and saw the fulfilled expressions of those who were receiving this new *sadhana* from Baba. How I craved to receive it. But no positive response came, and after waiting a few more days in vain, I returned to Jaipur.

Despite this disappointment, I still had hopes that my turn would come one day. Then I learnt that Bhatiji, our *bhukti pradhan* (the local unit head of Ananda Marga), had been called to Calcutta. He left at a moment's notice. Then, only two days later my brother informed me that I had also been called to receive the *microvita sadhana*.

Without bothering about a railway reservation I rushed to catch the fastest train to Calcutta. On reaching there, I found that Bhatiji was still waiting for his turn. In any case, I registered my presence and once again began to wait in the meditation hall from early morning till late at night. My brother would bring a packed lunch for me, which I used to gulp down in the hall itself. Again it was hope and hopelessness through which I passed for about three or four days. Then finally, Bhatiji was called in. My hopes now were raised.

After about half an hour Bhatiji came back from Baba's room. However, on my enquiry, he informed me that Baba was not happy about the way he did *sashtang pranam*, and therefore he had not been given the *microvita sadhana*. But Bhatiji was a very optimistic man. He resolved to learn the proper technique and was confident that he would be given another chance. My talk with him revealed that I was in the same boat as he, as I did not know how to do *sashtang pranam* and *pranayam* properly. So I resolved to correct myself. Thankfully, Acharya Vijayanandji Avadhuta took both Bhatiji and me under his wing and taught us the correct process of these practices. Later on it dawned on me that Baba had kept Bhatiji waiting until my arrival and returned him without giving him the *sadhana* for my benefit specially.

Then some days later Bhatiji was called again. This perhaps had not been done before or after, and he was given the *microvita sadhana*. All the *margiis* in Rajasthan know how he was transformed after this initiation.

Late in the evening one day my brother received a telephonic message that I was to present myself the next morning at six o'clock at Baba's residence. I became overjoyed on hearing the news and could hardly sleep that night. The next morning I was up before four and after taking my bath and doing morning *sadhana*, was at Lake Garden before five. I was ushered into Baba's room exactly at six.

Baba was sitting on his bed in a *lungi* and *banyan*. The room was pleasantly cool and a divine fragrance wafted all around. It was a spacious but sparsely furnished room. Just below his cot a blanket was spread, where I prostrated myself before him. I was in an incredible state of eagerness and joy. It occurred to me again and again that I was alone with Baba. Me and my master, and no one else! I sat down in front of him in the prescribed posture, my body bare above the waist. He was no more than three feet away from me.

'Have you had some spiritual experiences before or did you feel the presence of God sometimes', Baba asked. In that moment, somehow, I could not recollect anything. Then he said, 'Once, while reading in Pilani you were expelled from college. You fell seriously ill and the doctor told your family that you would not survive the night'. Baba went on to describe the entire incident and reminded me of the inner voice that had mysteriously helped me discard my near-fatal illness and regain my health. 'Was it not so? Who was ordering you from within?' he probed gently. Although I had been unaware of it, he was there with me on my deathbed when I was brought back to life.

Thereafter, he recalled my experience during *Navratra* when the meaning of the Gita's verse on the 'Knower' had become alive within me. Again, I came to realise that this blissful experience, which brought about a profound transformation in me, was only made possible by my guru. In this way, Baba reminded me of the pre-established harmony that existed between him and me.

As he proceeded to instruct me in the process of *microvita sadhana*, I was all attention to him and tried my best to follow.

I must maintain the secrecy of the process of initiation. It is doubly necessary; firstly, to maintain the tradition, and secondly, to avoid others copying the process from my record of the same, for the process differs from person to person and blind imitation may prove harmful in some way to those for whom it is not meant. Spiritual initiation is specific to the person concerned and involves much more than what can be stated in words. Each mind is unique in a hundred ways and only a guru who is competent to see deep into one's mind can prescribe exercises suitable for it. Initiation is not a type design that anyone can use, nor is it applicable universally.

Nevertheless, I pray for indulgence from my guru and seek his permission to state only a small part of the process that was of such incalculable significance to me. I realise that it is difficult to express the experience. Knowledge can be conveyed and communicated but not the experience. Yet, I should make an attempt to do the impossible for the sake of *jagathitaya*, the benefit of all seekers of truth.

To begin, Baba instructed me to inhale and exhale in a particular manner. I was to inhale loudly, so that he who was sitting about a yard away would also hear the sound, and was to exhale so quietly that even I could not hear a sound. And there was to be no gap between inhaling and exhaling, no retention of the breath, so loudly taken in and so quietly let out. Simple! It seemed so. But it was an arduous uphill climb.

I tried again and again but always failed. Sometimes, I would accidentally retain my breath briefly before exhaling, at other times I was not making enough sound while inhaling or was in a hurry to complete the exercise. I had to do the inhaling and exhaling for a prescribed number of times. Each time I failed, I began all over again and had to recite the *ishta* mantra also for a prescribed number of times before doing so. The more I failed the higher became this prescribed number. Whenever I thought I had completed the whole process correctly, Baba would point out that I had retained my breath longer than necessary or that he had heard me exhaling. I would agree with him and begin again.

Throughout the whole process, my eyes were closed, but I could feel Baba within my mind. It was abundantly clear to me that Baba was not only sitting outside of me, but was very much within me and more watchful of my breathing than I myself was. Gradually, it became a joint venture for both of us to do this *pranayam* correctly, exactly as per his instructions. With every breath, we became more and more intermingled in our common attempt to attain perfection. Now, not only did he point out my defects, but I too realised that I was not coming up to the standard.

I had never been in one posture — particularly in *siddhasana* — for so long. My legs became numb and distracted my attention. But he seemed unaware of this. I applied mental and physical force and although many a time I had an impulse to unlock the posture and straighten my legs, I continued sitting in the same posture. The blood supply to my legs would stop and resume again and the numbness would disappear. Somehow I managed to remain in that one posture for about three hours or more. Baba gave me the strength that day.

But my difficulty with breathing correctly continued and I began to feel that, perhaps, I would never be successful in my attempts. So much time had been wasted and I was still nowhere near the goal. By now I was in a state of utter hopelessness, while Baba was in a state of some irritation. Finally, I was about to give up, thinking that any moment now I would be sent out like Bhatiji to learn *pranayam* properly or worse never to be called back in again. My 'I' seemed like it was melting in a sea of grief and the fear of rejection gripped me.

While I was distracted by these feelings, I became unaware of what was happening within me, but when I concentrated once more on my breathing it had become perfect. It appeared that Baba had slipped from the seat of a watcher and instructor and taken the role of the doer. Now he was breathing and I was watching and the breathing had become perfect. A feeling of ecstasy surged within me. My grief was imperceptibly transposed into pure joy. It was he who was breathing within my body and I had become a superfluous observer who had only to watch and appreciate.

It is stated in the *shastras* that our being and the Almighty are like two birds sitting on the branch of the same fruit laden tree. One is eating the fruit and the other is enjoying this sight. One is the actor and the other the spectator. Using this metaphor the Upanishad explains the relationship of the *atman* with the *paramatman*, the relationshsip of the soul with the Supreme.

But the scriptures do not say that sometimes the roles are swapped. Saint Tulsidasji says that 'He alone knows him whom he manifests himself and after this (knowledge) both become one and non-dual'.

I don't know whether my experience fits in with this description. But the realisation that it is *he* who is breathing in my body gives me a strange sensation of peace and love.

Breathing is the most vital and physical of all the functions of our being. Constant awareness of breathing is prescribed as a spiritual practice in *vipassana*, a Buddhist form of meditation. But Baba gave me something more than simple awareness of breathing. He made me realise that it is he who is breathing within my body. But is this body mine then? No, it would be a mistake to own this body where the breather is someone else! The net result seems to be that the 'I' feeling is surplus and superfluous. Who but a *sadguru* can give this feeling, which is no longer a concept, nor knowledge, nor an imagination, but a real experience? No doubt, he is me or I am him — which is a more correct expression? He alone knows! Perhaps, confirmation of this truth or the actual experience of this reality was a necessary prerequisite for my initiation into *microvita sadhana*.

When one attains salvation, one's small 'I' merges into the great 'I' of the vast Purusa. Originating from the mountain caves, crossing countless valleys and green and golden plains, the mountain river finally merges with the blue water of the sea. Does that river really die? No, it does not die. There is no permanent death of any entity. The rhythmic sweetness of rivers lives eternally in the surging waves of the vast oceans. Although people know this, they want to forget it. And because they remain oblivious to this fact, they become overwhelmed with sorrow. In fact, all entities are living eternally in supreme blessedness within the vast bosom of the Supreme Entity ... Nothing is lost, nothing was lost, nothing ever will be lost.

30 July 1982, Patna

Return to Jamalpur

It was somewhat of a painful and difficult decision to pay another visit to Jamalpur in 1996 in the physical absence of my guru. A long railway journey always proves a setback to my health at this advanced age. Train journeys generally involve waterless fasting, as the eatables available on the way are so oily, spicy and polluted, and even reliable potable water is scarce. Even so, I could not resist the temptation of reviewing all the sweet memories of Baba, to see his room once more and relive the walks and long sittings on the tiger's grave, and to recollect those miracles that used to happen so spontaneously and frequently during my stays there.

On this journey, I travelled with my grandson, Pranav, who was keen to visit Jamalpur for the first time. Our train, as usual, was five hours late and instead of reaching at around noon we arrived there in the evening. As on my first visit to Jamalpur, we were informed that the venue of the function was at Munger and so should continue on to there. But the function was only of secondary importance for me, my first priority being Jamalpur, that almost anonymous little town in the state of Bihar, which had given so much meaning and sustenance to thousands around the world.

So my grandson and I decided to stay in the retiring rooms at the Jamalpur station. After unpacking our luggage we were informed that the water supply in the room was disrupted due to some fault in the pumping station. So to freshen up we had to make do with two small bucketfuls of water that had been stored in the bathroom. What we were very much in need of was a long cool shower, but instead we got only a quarter of a bath each. Perhaps this physical inconvenience was again necessary to prepare my mind for the spiritual feast we were to enjoy shortly.

We rushed to the field and tiger's grave before it became too dark. The evening breeze was cool and as the night advanced it become so cold that by 9:30pm I had already developed a cold. We met troops of *sanyasis* returning from the field. They pointed us in the right direction, as in the course of a thirty-year gap, I had lost my moorings in this place with which I was once so familiar. We sat reverentially on the tiger's grave and the past began to appear on my mental plate as if in a movie reel. It was here that I developed that eternal bond with my master, which is now the staple of my existence. We prolonged our stay in the field as long as possible, doing *sadhana* and talking of Baba to our heart's content. The moonless night had advanced a lot by the time we came back to the retiring rooms. For dinner we had cups of milk and pieces of bread from the railway restaurant downstairs.

The next morning there was a lot of sweet irresistible pressure to move to a *margii's* house. We succumbed to it and found that Prakashji's small house was already overflowing with relatives and guests who had come to attend the congregation in Munger. However small the size of the house, it was more than compensated for by the largeness of the hearts of the hosts, who left no stones unturned to make us feel comfortable. We were soon joined there by the Khullars from Delhi and Rajpal Singhji from Jaipur. The place was infested with swarms of mosquitoes, but our hosts were able to provide giant mosquito nets to protect every guest from their bites. The food was sentient and tasty, and we enjoyed five-star hospitality in that small place.

We spent the day in Munger, attending the discourse by the new spiritual head of Ananda Marga, meeting people from different parts of the country and exchanging our experiences of the past and present. In the evening, again before it became dark, some of us proceeded towards the field and the tiger's grave.

A blissful breeze was blowing from the hills and transporting me into the past, reminding me of when I used to spend the first part of the night in the heavenly company of my guru. Someone among us sang a *Prabhat*

Sangeet, then we sang *kirtan* together and did meditation. When the stars began to twinkle prominently in the dark moonless night, we prepared to return to our residence.

But as we were about to leave, two people were seen to approach the grave; one of them was tall and wore pants and a shirt, the other was short and clad in a white *dhoti* and *kurta*. They enquired whether they could join us. It was too dark to see each other's faces properly and there was some difficulty in conversation, as both of them were Bengali speaking while we were all from the north-west of India and not so familiar with Bengali. However, soon it became clear that the short one out of the two arrivals wished to sing *Prabhat Sangeet.*

He began hesitatingly, but soon his melodious voice reverberated throughout the field, the valley and the hills. We were spellbound by the beauty of his voice, and the tenderness and longing brought tears to everyone's eyes. Even my grandson, who did not understand much of the songs' meaning, did not remain dry-eyed. One song after another, the blissful singing continued for over an hour. Thereafter came the turn of the man's taller companion who sang *kiirtan* in different tunes. We followed this with another round of meditation. When finally we got up and began to disperse, the most unexpected thing happened.

As we were saying our goodbyes, we introduced ourselves to one another. When the short fellow heard my name, he looked greatly surprised, and embraced me with much love and affection. He explained with excitement that long, long ago Baba had told him he should learn to speak Hindi from Mangal Bihari and in return he should teach Mangal Bihari Bengali. He had been sitting with Baba on the tiger's grave and on asking Baba when and where he could meet me, Baba replied, 'Hereabouts, someday'. This was during the time when Baba used to live in Jamalpur and would deliver his talks and discourses in Hindi. Remembering Baba's words now the short man felt fulfilled that after all these years they had come true. I in turn was utterly surprised and felt exceptionally blessed to hear this story from a stranger who came from a small village in the remote interior of Bengal. It strengthened my belief that Baba was still with me, though he was not physically present. Now I realised what had pulled me to Jamalpur so strongly, despite the prospects of a long and tiring journey. I could not but come here, as Baba's words had to be fulfilled for that unknown devotee.

The following day we visited five or six residences in the town and the railway colony, where Baba had stayed from time to time while he was in Jamalpur. We also saw the Shiva temple, where at the age of four the young Prabhat Ranjan had gone with his father and recited the *Shiva Stuti* in such chaste and clear Sanskrit, although none in the family or temple had heard it before. We climbed up the hill and saw the death valley, or what remains of it now. What was once a dense forest, is now nothing but small bushes and patches of barren stone, due to the indiscriminate felling of trees. The field itself, which used to be lush green in those days, is only an open space now.

Nevertheless, it was in these places that Prabhat Ranjan, my beloved Baba, used to come as a child, and spend his nights or the better part of them in solitary splendour. The two graves of the tiger and the Englishman stand silently, as a most precious treasure of a thousand memories.

Tell everyone, all my sons and daughters,
that I am yours. I love each and every particle
of this universe. My love is for everyone.
I am always with you.

Unknown Caller

A couple of years ago, I went to get a heart check-up in Delhi. Three months earlier I had undergone a heart bypass surgery. Lately I was experiencing problems with the blood circulation in my legs. But at the Escorts hospital the cost of correcting the circulation in one leg was Rs. 2.3 *lakhs*, which was a bit beyond my means.

The late Vice President of India, Bhairon Singh Shekhawat, was a good friend of mine, and when he came to know about my health, he called the Director of the All India Institute of Medical Sciences (AIIMS) in Delhi, requesting him to take a look at my case. Normally it took about two months to even get an appointment at this prestigious medical institution, which being government owned, treated patients free of charge. The

Director saw me the following day and after examining me came to the conclusion that despite the seriousness of my condition it would be preferable to avoid further surgery due to my advanced age.

After returning to Jaipur my condition deteriorated further. I lost my appetite and ran a constant fever. Initially the local doctor treated my condition as a viral fever. When this treatment did not have any effect I was diagnosed with malaria and was given heavy doses of quinine. All in all the treatment continued for around fifteen days, but my condition got worse. I couldn't move and my body had become extremely weak due to the lack of food intake. Finally, one night I became very restless and had great difficulty in breathing. By midnight my condition was so serious that my son took me to the nearest hospital.

This was a small hospital, which was just a kilometer away from our house. I had been there once before. On that occasion, there was only a trainee doctor to attend to me who did not seem to understand much about my condition. We had left the hospital disappointed and sought another doctor.

This time we reached the hospital at around midnight. As I stumbled out of my car, I was astonished to see that there was a large team waiting to receive me at the hospital entrance. The sentry and the ward boy immediately sat me on a wheelchair and rushed me to the intensive care unit on the third floor. There, surprisingly, the owner of the hospital, himself a heart specialist, was awaiting me with a team of specialists and nurses. They were on my case as soon as I entered the ICU and within thirty to forty minutes my condition stabilised. I was given oxygen and the necessary medicines via drip and soon fell asleep.

In the morning when I awoke I found the Head Compounder next to my bed. He congratulated me on making it to the hospital in the nick of time. Only a few minutes delay and it would very likely have been too late. I breathed a deep sigh of relief and enquired how it was that they were all present and prepared at that time of night. It was then that the mystery was unravelled.

At 11 o'clock an anonymous call from the Governor's house had informed the hospital of the imminent arrival of a very important official needing treatment. The hospital chief had all his key specialists ready and waiting and when they saw me arriving they concluded that I must be the important official. Later they called the Governor's house several times, but could not ascertain who had made the call.

While they were perplexed about the unknown caller, my eyes filled with tears of love and gratitude for Baba. To me this was his immense grace. Through an anonymous telephone call he had made excellent arrangements for my treatment. Though he has left his physical body, his companionship with his devotees is eternal.

Our visit to the Ananda Marga Sectorial Conference in Germany, 2000

Acknowledgements

This book is neither a narrative nor even strictly chronological. My plan was to give a thorough and comprehensive view of my inner self before and after I met my guru, P. R. Sarkar. But I began rather late in life and did not work with the needed focus and diligence. From the numerous episodes that deserved to be told, I have only been able to re-collect a selection of impressions. As I grew older my memory began to fade and decay. Well-wishers advised me to get into print whatever had already been written. I leaned on my grandson, Pranav, and his wife, Kalyanii, to arrange and edit the matter. The result is before you.

I would like to extend my gratitude to Dada Jyotirupananda who lent his eyes to go through the messy text and weed out many errors. Thanks also to Julian Towsey who helped with proof-reading.

Dr Sohail Inayatullah kindly agreed to provide an overview and context for the book and my sincere thanks to him for doing a fine job with that. He has been such an articulate exponent of Baba's works. Dada Yatiishvarananda was very generous in writing the foreword and I will always appreciate the friendship we have shared over the years.

Need I mention again that without Pranav and Kalyanii's undertaking to edit and publish these scattered impressions, this book would not have been possible.

I do not know how to thank one person though — my loving and patient companion for seven decades and one who has shared this spiritual journey with me at every step. Sarla, my wife, continues to be an enormous pillar of support and strength. Her simple and steadfast devotion for Baba is deeply inspirational.

www.ingramcontent.com/pod-product-compliance
Ingram Content Group UK Ltd.
Pitfield, Milton Keynes, MK11 3LW, UK
UKHW020222250726
13967UKWH00001B/147

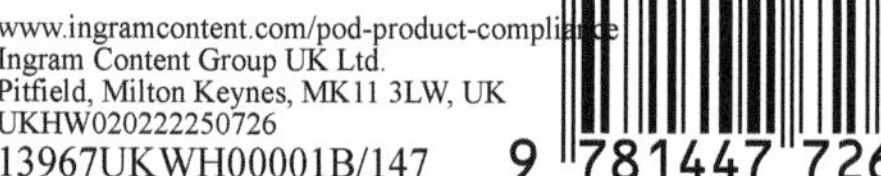

9 781447 726050